The
POWER
of the
BLOOD

The POWER *of the* BLOOD

The Vital Role of Blood for Redemption, Sanctification, and Life

ANDREW MURRAY

We love hearing from our readers. Please contact us at www.anekopress.com/questions-comments with any questions, comments, or suggestions.

Cover Design: Natalia Hawthorne, BookCoverLabs.com
Cover Photography: Maria Dryfhout/Shutterstock
eBook Icon: Icons Vector/Shutterstock
Editors: Sheila Wilkinson and Ruth Zetek
Printed in the United States of America

Aneko Press – *Our Readers Matter*™
www.anekopress.com
Aneko Press, Life Sentence Publishing, and our logos are trademarks of Life Sentence Publishing, Inc.
203 E. Birch Street
P.O. Box 652
Abbotsford, WI 54405
RELIGION / Christian Theology / Christology
Paperback ISBN: 978-1-62245-372-6
eBook ISBN: 978-1-62245-373-3
10 9 8 7 6 5 4 3 2 1
Available where books are sold

Contents

Preface

This book is a translation of portions of messages by my late father, Reverend Andrew Murray, MA, DD, on *The Power of the Blood of Jesus*, which so far have appeared only in Dutch.

The translator is the Rev. William M. Douglas, BA, who was my father's intimate friend and associated with him in connection with the South African Keswick Convention Movement for many years. During my father's lifetime, he permitted Mr. Douglas to translate his book *The Prayer Life*, and after my father's death, Mr. Douglas became his biographer.

After reading this manuscript, I believe the translation is excellent. He has reproduced the thoughts of my father exactly.

I am certain blessings will result from the prayerful and thoughtful reading of these chapters.

Trusting you may learn to value and live in the experience of the power of the precious blood of our Lord and Savior Jesus Christ, I remain,

Yours in the Blessed Master's service,

M. E. Murray

Clairvaux

Wellington, C. P., South Africa.

Chapter 1

What the Scriptures Teach about the Blood

Not without blood (Hebrews 9:7)

G od has spoken to us in the Scriptures in numerous parts and in various manners, but the voice is always the same – it is the Word of the same God.

For that reason, treating the Bible as a whole and receiving the witness it gives in its various portions concerning definite truths is essential. In this way we can recognize the place these truths occupy in the heart of God. We can discover the foundational truths of the Bible, which demand attention more than others do. These truths stand prominently with each new development in God's revelation; they remain unchanged when the dispensation changes, and they carry a divine suggestion of their importance.

In the following chapters, my objective is to show what the Scriptures teach us about the glorious power of the blood of Jesus and the wonderful blessings secured for us. I cannot lay a better foundation for my exposition or give a better proof of the matchless glory of that blood as the power of redemption than by asking my readers to follow along through the Bible. We will see the unique place that is given to the blood from the beginning to the end of God's revelation of Himself to man as recorded in the Bible.

Clearly, no single scriptural theme from Genesis to Revelation is kept in view more consistently and prominently than that expressed by the words *the blood.*

Our study, then, is what the Scriptures teach us about the blood:

1. In the Old Testament.

2. In the teaching of our Lord Jesus.

3. In the teaching of the apostles.

4. In the book of Revelation.

Blood in the Old Testament

The record about the blood begins at the gates of Eden, but I will not investigate the unrevealed mysteries of Eden.

The connection of blood with Abel's sacrifice, however, is plain to see. He *brought of the firstborn of his flock* to the Lord as a sacrifice; there, in connection with the first act of worship recorded in the Bible, blood was shed (Genesis 4:4). We learn from Hebrews 11:4 that it was *by faith* that Abel offered an acceptable sacrifice, and his name appears first in the record of those whom the Bible calls believers. *By faith Abel offered unto God a more excellent sacrifice than Cain, by which he obtained witness that he was righteous* (Hebrews 11:4). So, Abel's faith and God's good pleasure in him are closely connected with the sacrificial blood.

In light of later revelation, this testimony, given at the very beginning of human history, is of deep significance. It shows that there can be no approach to God, no fellowship with Him by faith, and no enjoyment of His favor apart from blood.

Scripture gives little detail of the next sixteen centuries, but then came the flood, which was God's judgment on sin by the destruction of the world of mankind. But God brought forth a new earth from that dreadful baptism of water.

Notice, however, that the new earth was also baptized with blood, and the first recorded act of Noah after he had left the ark was the offering of a burnt sacrifice to God. As with Abel in the beginning, so with Noah at a new beginning, connection with God was *not without blood.*

Sin once again prevailed, however, and God laid an entirely new foundation for the establishment of His kingdom on earth. By the divine call of Abram and the miraculous birth of Isaac, God chose a people to serve Him, but His purpose was not accomplished apart from the shedding of the blood. This is apparent in the most solemn hour of Abraham's life.

God had already entered into a covenant relationship with Abraham, and his faith had already been severely tried, and he had stood the test.

> *And he did not weaken in faith: he considered not*
> *his own body now dead when he was about one*
> *hundred years old, neither yet the deadness of Sara's*
> *womb; he doubted not the promise of God, with*
> *unbelief, but was strengthened in faith, giving glory*
> *to God, being fully persuaded that he was also pow-*
> *erful to do all that he had promised; therefore, his*
> *faith was also attributed unto him as righteousness.*
> (Romans 4:19-22)

It was reckoned, or counted to him, for righteousness. *For what does the scripture say? Abraham believed God, and it was counted unto him for righteousness* (Romans 4:3). Yet, Abraham had to learn that Isaac, the son of promise, who belonged wholly to God, could be truly surrendered to God only by death.

Isaac had to die. For Abraham, as well as for Isaac, only by death could freedom from the self-life be obtained. Abraham had to offer Isaac on the altar. That was not an arbitrary command of God. It was the revelation of a divine truth – it is only through death that a life truly consecrated to God is possible. So, *by faith Abraham, when he was tried, offered up Isaac, and he that had received the promises offered up his only begotten son, of whom it was said, That in Isaac shall thy seed be called, accounting that God was able to raise him up, even from the dead; from whence he also received him in a figure* (Hebrews 11:17-19).

But it was impossible for Isaac to die and rise again from the dead; because of sin, death would hold him fast. *And Abraham lifted up his eyes and looked and beheld behind him a ram caught in a thicket by his horns; and Abraham went and took the ram and offered him up for a burnt offering instead of his son* (Genesis 22:13). Isaac's life was spared, and a ram was offered in his place. Through the blood that then flowed on Mount Moriah, Isaac's life was spared. He and his descendants live before God but *not without blood.* By that blood, he was figuratively raised again from the dead. The great lesson of substitution is clearly taught here.

Four hundred years pass, and Isaac's descendants have become the people of Israel in Egypt. Through her deliverance from Egyptian bondage, Israel became recognized as God's firstborn among the nations. *Thou shalt say unto Pharaoh, The LORD hath said thus: Israel is my son, even my firstborn* (Exodus 4:22). Once again, it is *not without blood.* Neither the grace of God, nor His covenant with Abraham, nor the exercise of His omnipotence, which could have destroyed their oppressors, could dispense with the necessity of the blood.

What the blood accomplished on Mount Moriah for one

person, Abraham, who was the father of the nation, now had to be experienced by that nation. By the sprinkling of the doorframes of the Israelites with the blood of the Paschal Lamb and the institution of the Passover as an enduring ordinance, the people were taught that life could be obtained only by the death of a substitute. *This blood shall be to you for a sign upon the houses where ye are; and when I see the blood, I will pass over you, and the plague shall not be upon you to destroy you, when I smite the land of Egypt* (Exodus 12:13). Life was possible for them only through the blood of a life given in their place and appropriated by the sprinkling of the blood. *By faith he* [Moses] *kept the passover and the sprinkling of the blood lest he that destroyed the firstborn should touch them* (Hebrews 11:28).

In the third month, this lesson was enforced in a striking manner. Israel had reached Sinai and God had given His law as the foundation of His covenant. That covenant now had to be established, and as stated in Hebrews 9:7, *not without blood*. Moses sprinkled the sacrificial blood on the altar and then on the book of the covenant, representing God's side of that covenant; then he sprinkled it on the people with the declaration, *Behold the blood of the covenant, which the LORD has made with you concerning all these words* (Exodus 24:8; Hebrews 9:19).

The covenant had its foundation and power in that blood, and by it alone, God and man can be brought into covenant fellowship. That which had been foreshadowed at the gate of Eden, on Mount Ararat, on Moriah, and in Egypt was now confirmed at the foot of Sinai in a most solemn manner. Without blood there could be no access by sinful man to a holy God.

There is, however, a marked difference between the manner of applying the blood in the former cases as compared to the latter. On Moriah, the life was redeemed by the shedding of the blood. In Egypt, it was sprinkled on the doorposts of the houses, but at Sinai, it was sprinkled on the persons themselves. The contact was closer, the application more powerful.

Immediately after the establishment of the covenant, the command was given, *Let them make me a sanctuary, that I may dwell among them* (Exodus 25:8). They were to enjoy the full blessedness of having the God of the covenant abiding among them. Through His grace they could find Him and serve Him in His house.

He Himself gave, with the minutest care, directions for the arrangement and service of that house. Imagine yourself in this temple; you notice that the blood is the center and reason for all of this. Draw near to the vestibule of the earthly temple of the heavenly King, and the first thing visible is the altar of burnt offering, where the sprinkling of blood continues without ceasing from morning until evening. Enter the Holy Place, and the most conspicuous thing is the golden altar of incense, which is constantly sprinkled with the blood. Ask what lies beyond the Holy Place, and you will be told that it is the most Holy Place where God dwells. If you ask how He dwells there, and how He is approached, you will be told *not without blood.* The golden throne where His glory shines is itself sprinkled with the blood once every year, when the high priest alone enters to bring in the blood and to worship God. The highest act in that worship is the sprinkling of the blood.

If you inquire further, you will be told that always and for everything the blood is the one necessary thing. The way to fellowship with God is through the blood alone – at the consecration of the house or of the priests, at the birth of a child, in the deepest repentance of sin, in the highest festival, and in everything.

This continued for fifteen hundred years. At Sinai, in the desert, at Shiloh, and in the temple on Mount Moriah it continued until our Lord came to fulfill and thereby make an end of all shadows or types by bringing in the substance and establishing a fellowship with the Holy One in spirit and truth.

Blood in the Teaching of Our Lord Jesus

With the coming of Jesus, old things passed away, and all things became new. He came from the Father in heaven and can tell us in divine words the way to the Father.

Sometimes we are told that the words *not without blood* belong to the Old Testament. But what does our Lord Jesus Christ say? First notice that when John the Baptist announced His coming, he spoke of Him as filling a dual office: *the Lamb of God, who takes away the sin of the world* and then *he who baptizes with the Holy Spirit* (John 1:29, 33). The outpouring of the blood of the Lamb of God had to take place before the outpouring of the Spirit could be given. Only when all that the Old Testament taught about the blood had been fulfilled could the Spirit begin its work.

The Lord Jesus Christ plainly declared that His death on the cross was the purpose for which He came into the world; His death was the means of the redemption and life that He came to bring. He clearly states that the shedding of His blood was necessary in His death.

In the synagogue at Capernaum, Jesus spoke of Himself as *the bread of life* that He would give for the life of the world (John 6:35). Four times He said most emphatically, *Unless ye . . . drink his blood, ye shall have no life in you. . . . Whosoever . . . drinks my blood has eternal life, . . . my blood is drink indeed. He that . . . drinks my blood abides in me, and I in him* (John 6:53-56).[1] Our Lord thus declared the fundamental fact that He,

---

1   Literal drinking of blood was forbidden in Jewish law, so we know that John is speaking figuratively here (Leviticus 17:14). According to the NAS Greek Lexicon, the figurative definition of the word *drink* is "to receive into the soul what serves to refresh, strengthen, and nourish it unto eternal life." *www. biblestudytools.com/lexicons/greek/nas/ pino.html.*

as the Son of the Father who came to restore our lost life to us, can do this in no other way than by dying for us – by shedding His blood for us and making us partakers of its power.

Our Lord confirmed the teaching of the Old Testament offerings – that man can only live through the death of another and thus obtain a life that through resurrection has become eternal.

But Christ Himself cannot make us partakers of that eternal life, which He has obtained for us, except by the shedding of His blood and causing us to drink it. Marvelous fact! *Not without blood* can eternal life be ours.

Equally striking is our Lord's declaration of the same truth on the last night of His earthly life. Before He completed the great work of His life by giving it as *a ransom for many,* He took the cup at the Last Supper, saying *this is my blood of the new testament, which is shed for many for the remission of sins* (Matthew 26:28). *Without shedding of blood there is no remission* [of sins] (Hebrews 9:22). Without remission of sins there is no life. But by the shedding of His blood, He has obtained a new life for us. By what He calls the *drinking of His blood,* He shares His life with us. The blood, which was shed in the atonement, frees us from the guilt of sin and from death, the punishment of sin. The blood, which by faith we receive into our soul, gives us His life. The blood He shed was first *for* us and then given *to* us.

Blood in the Teaching of the Apostles

After His resurrection and ascension, our Lord is no longer known by the apostles after the flesh. *Therefore from now on we know no one according to the flesh: and even if we have known Christ according to the flesh, yet now we know him no longer* (2 Corinthians 5:16). Now, all that was symbolic has passed away, and the deep spiritual truths expressed by symbol are unveiled.

But there is no veiling of the blood. It still occupies a

prominent place. The epistle to the Hebrews was written purposely to show that the temple service had become unprofitable, and God intended it to pass away now that Christ had come.

Here, if anywhere, it might be expected that the Holy Spirit would emphasize the true spirituality of God's purpose, yet it is here that a new value is given to the phrase *the blood of Jesus.*

We read concerning our Lord that *by his own blood he entered in once into the sanctuary designed for eternal redemption* (Hebrews 9:12).

How much more shall the blood of the Christ, who through the eternal Spirit offered himself without spot to God, purge your conscience from the works of death to serve the living God? (Hebrews 9:14)

Having therefore, brethren, boldness to enter into the sanctuary by the blood of Jesus. (Hebrews 10:19)

Ye are come . . . to Jesus, the mediator of the new testament and to the blood of sprinkling, that speaks better than that of Abel. (Hebrews 12:22, 24)

Jesus also, that he might sanctify the people with his own blood, suffered outside the camp. (Hebrews 13:12)

Now the God of peace, that brought again from the dead our Lord Jesus, that great shepherd of the sheep, through the blood of the eternal testament. (Hebrews 13:20)

By such words the Holy Spirit teaches us that the blood is the central power of our entire redemption. *Not without blood* is as valid in the New Testament as in the Old. Nothing but the blood of Jesus, shed in His death for sin, can cover sin on God's side or remove it on ours.

We find the same teaching in the writings of the apostles.

Paul writes of *being justified freely by his grace through the redemption that is in Jesus, the Christ, whom God purposed for reconciliation through faith in his blood* (Romans 3:24-25). Later Paul writes, *much more now justified in his blood, we shall be saved from wrath by him* (Romans 5:9).

To the Corinthians he declares that *the cup of blessing which we bless, is it not the fellowship of the blood of the Christ?* (1 Corinthians 10:16).

In the epistle to the Galatians, Paul uses the word *cross* to convey the same meaning, while in Colossians he unites the two words and speaks of *the blood of his cross* (Galatians 6:14; Colossians 1:20).

He reminds the Ephesians that *we have redemption through his blood* and that we *are made near by the blood of the Christ* (Ephesians 1:7; 2:13).

Peter reminds his readers that they were *chosen . . . to obey and be sprinkled with the blood of Jesus, the Christ* (1 Peter 1:2). He said they were redeemed *with the precious blood of the Christ* (1 Peter 1:19).

See how John assures his *little children* that *the blood of Jesus Christ, his Son cleanses us from all sin* (1 John 1:7). The Son is *Jesus, the Christ, who came by water and blood; not by water only, but by water and blood* (1 John 5:6).

By glorying in the blood, all of them agree that the power for eternal redemption through Christ is fully accomplished and is then applied by the Holy Spirit.

But perhaps this is merely earthly language. What does heaven say? What do we learn from future glory?

Blood in the Book of Revelation

It is of greatest importance to notice that in the book of Revelation where God describes the glory of His throne and the blessedness of those who surround it, the blood retains its prominent place.

On the throne John saw *a Lamb as it had been slain* (Revelation 5:6). As the elders fell down before the Lamb, they sang a new song: *Thou art worthy . . . for thou wast slain and hast redeemed us unto God by thy blood* (Revelation 5:9).

Later, when he saw the great company, which no man could number, he was told who they were: *These are those who came out of great tribulation and have washed their long robes, and made them white in the blood of the Lamb* (Revelation 7:14).

Then again, John heard the song of victory over the defeat of Satan: *They have overcome him by the blood of the Lamb* (Revelation 12:11).

In the glory of heaven, as seen by John, there was no phrase by which the great purposes of God, the wondrous love of the Son of God, or the power of His redemption and the joy and thanksgiving of the redeemed can be gathered up and expressed except this: *the blood of the Lamb.* From the beginning to the end of Scripture, from the closing of the gates of Eden to the opening of the gates of the heavenly Jerusalem, there runs a golden thread: the blood unites the beginning and the end and gloriously restores what sin had destroyed.

It is not difficult to see what lessons the Lord wishes us to learn from the fact that the blood occupies such a prominent place in Scripture.

God Has No Other Way of Dealing with Sin or the Sinner Except Through the Blood

For victory over sin and the deliverance of the sinner, God has provided no other means or thought than the blood of Christ. Yes, it is indeed something that surpasses all understanding.

All the wonders of grace are focused in the blood:

> The incarnation, by which He took upon Himself
> our flesh and blood (John 1:14)

The love that spared not itself but surrendered itself to death (Romans 5:8)

The righteousness, the forgiveness by redemption through his blood (Ephesians 1:7)

The substitution, the righteous One atoned for the unrighteous (2 Corinthians 5:21)

The atonement for sin (Hebrews 2:17)

The justification made possible renewed fellowship with God (2 Corinthians 5:18)

The cleansing and sanctification to fit us for that fellowship (Ephesians 5:25-27)

The true oneness in life with the Lord Jesus, as He gives His life (John 17:11, 21)

The eternal joy of the hymn of praise, *Thou . . . hast redeemed us unto God* (Revelation 5:9)

All these are but rays of the wondrous light, which are reflected upon us from the precious blood of Jesus.

The Blood Must Have the Same Place in Our Hearts That It Has with God

From the beginning of God's dealings with man, from before the foundation of the world, the heart of God has rejoiced in the blood of Jesus. Our heart will never rest, nor find salvation, until we also learn to walk and glory in the power of that blood.

The penitent sinner longing for pardon is not the only one who must value the blood of Jesus. No, the redeemed will also experience that yearning as God sits upon the throne of grace in His temple, where the blood is always evident. Nothing draws our hearts closer to God and fills them with His love and joy and glory as living in constant, spiritual view of that blood.

Let Us Take Time and Trouble to Learn the Full Blessing and Power of That Blood

The blood of Jesus is the greatest mystery of eternity, the deepest mystery of the divine wisdom. Let's not imagine that we can easily grasp its meaning. God thought four thousand years was necessary to prepare men for it, and we also must take time, if we are to gain a knowledge of the power of the blood.

Even taking time is not enough, however, unless that taking involves sacrificial trouble. Sacrificial blood always meant the offering of a life. The Israelite could not obtain blood for the pardon of his sin unless the life of something that belonged to him was offered in sacrifice. The Lord Jesus did not offer up His own life and shed His blood to spare us from the sacrifice of our lives. No, indeed. He did it to make the sacrifice of our lives possible and desirable.

The hidden value of His blood is the spirit of self-sacrifice; where the blood really touches the heart, it works out in that heart a similar spirit of self-sacrifice. We learn to give ourselves and our lives to press into the power of that new life, which the blood has provided.

We give our time to become acquainted with these things in God's Word. We separate ourselves from sin, worldly-mindedness, and self-will, so the power of the blood may not be hindered, because it seeks to remove these things.

We surrender ourselves to God in prayer and faith, so we don't think our own thoughts or hold our own lives as a prize but as possessing nothing except what He gives. Then He reveals to us the glorious and blessed life that has been prepared for us by the blood.

We Can Rely upon the Lord Jesus to Reveal the Power of His Blood

By our confident trust in Him, the blessing obtained by the

blood becomes ours. We must never separate the blood from the High Priest who shed it and lives to apply it.

He, who once gave His blood for us, will impart its potential. Trust Him to do this. Trust Him to open your eyes and give you a deeper spiritual insight. Trust Him to teach you to think about the blood as God thinks about it. Trust Him to impart to you, and make effective in you, all that He enables you to see.

Trust Him above all, in the power of His eternal high priesthood, to work unceasingly in you the full merits of His blood, so that your whole life may be an uninterrupted abiding in the sanctuary of God's presence.

Believer, you who have come to the knowledge of the precious blood, hearken to the invitation of your Lord. Come nearer. Let Him teach you; let Him bless you. Let Him cause His blood to become spirit, and life, and power, and truth to you.

Begin now, at once, to open your soul in faith, to receive the full, mighty, heavenly effects of the precious blood in a more glorious manner than you have ever experienced. He Himself will work these things out in your life.

Chapter 2

Redemption by Blood

Knowing that ye have been ransomed . . . not with corruptible things like silver and gold, but with the precious blood of the Christ, as of a lamb without blemish and without contamination. (1 Peter 1:18-19)

The shedding of His blood was the culmination of the sufferings of our Lord. The atoning effectiveness of those sufferings was in that shed blood. Therefore, the believer should not be satisfied with the mere acceptance of the blessed truth that he is redeemed by that blood, but he should press on to a more complete knowledge of what is meant by that statement and learn what that blood is intended to do in a surrendered soul.

Its effects are manifold, for we read in Scripture of:

Reconciliation through the blood.

Cleansing through the blood.

Sanctification through the blood.

Union with God through the blood.

Victory over Satan through the blood.

Life through the blood.

These are separate blessings but are all included in one phrase: Redemption by the blood. Only when the believer understands these blessings and how they may become his can he experience the full power of redemption.

Before we consider the details of these several blessings, let's examine in a more general way the power of the blood of Jesus.

1. Where does the power of that blood lie?

2. What has that power accomplished?

3. How can we experience its effects?

Where Does the Power of the Blood Lie?

In other words, what is it that gives such power to the blood of Jesus? How is it that there is power in the blood alone that is possessed by nothing else?

The answer to this question is found in Leviticus: *For the soul (or life) of the flesh is in the blood, and I have given it to you to reconcile your persons (or souls) upon the altar; therefore the same blood reconciles the person* (Leviticus 17:11). It is because the *soul, or life, is in the blood,* and the blood is offered to God on the altar that it has in it redemptive power.

The soul or life is in the blood; therefore, the value of the blood corresponds to the value of the life that is in it. The life of a sheep or goat is of less value than the life of an ox, so the blood of a sheep or a goat in an offering is of less value than the blood of an ox (Leviticus 4).

The life of man is more valuable than that of many sheep or oxen. Now who can determine the value or the power of the blood of Jesus? In that blood dwelt the soul of the holy Son of God. The eternal life of the Godhead was carried in that blood, as can be seen by Paul's advice to the Ephesians: *Take heed therefore unto yourselves and to all the flock, in which the*

Holy Spirit has placed you as bishops to feed the congregation of God, which he has purchased with his own blood (Acts 20:28). The power of that blood in its various effects is nothing less than the eternal power of God Himself. What a glorious thought for everyone who desires to experience the full power of the blood!

But the power of the blood lies above everything else in the fact that it is offered to God on the altar for redemption. When we think of blood as shed, we think of death; death follows when the blood or the soul is poured out. Death makes us think of sin, for death is the punishment of sin. *For the wages of sin is death, but the grace of God is eternal life in Christ Jesus our Lord* (Romans 6:23). God gave Israel the blood on the altar as the atonement or covering for sin; that means the sins of the transgressor were laid on the victim, and its death was reckoned as the death or punishment for the sins laid upon it.

> *This shall be the law of sin: In the place where*
> *the burnt offering is killed shall the atonement as*
> *sin be killed before the LORD; for it is most holy.*
> (Leviticus 6:25)

The blood was thus the life given up to death for the satisfaction of the law of God and in obedience to His command. Sin was so entirely covered and atoned for, it was no longer reckoned as that of the transgressor. He was forgiven.

But all these sacrifices and offerings were only types and shadows until the Lord Jesus came. His blood was the reality to which these types pointed. *For he has made him to be sin for us, who knew no sin, that we might be made the righteousness of God in him* (2 Corinthians 5:21).

His blood was in itself of infinite value, because it carried His soul or life. But the atoning virtue of His blood was infinite also, because of the manner in which it was shed. In holy obedience to the Father's will, He subjected Himself to the penalty of the broken law by pouring out His soul unto death. By that death, not only was the penalty paid, but the law was also satisfied and the Father glorified. His blood atoned for sin and thus made it powerless. His blood has a marvelous power for removing sin and opening heaven for the sinner. It cleanses, and sanctifies, and makes him fit for heaven.

So why does the blood of Jesus have such wonderful power? Because Jesus was the wonderful Person whose blood was shed and because of the wonderful way in which it was shed. It fulfilled the law of God and satisfied its just demands. It is the blood of atonement and therefore is sufficient to redeem and accomplish everything for, and in, the sinner that is necessary to salvation.

What Has That Power Accomplished?

As we see the wonders of what that power has accomplished, we will be encouraged to believe that it can do the same for us. We can best see this in the examples in the Scriptures of the great things that have taken place through the power of the blood of Jesus.

The Blood of Jesus Has Opened the Grave

We read in Hebrews: *Now the God of peace, that brought again from the dead our Lord Jesus that great shepherd of the sheep, through the blood of the eternal testament* (Hebrews 13:20).

It was through the excellence of the blood that God raised Jesus from the dead. God's almighty power was not exerted apart from the blood.

He came to earth as a guarantee and a bearer of the sin of mankind. Through the shedding of His blood alone, He had the right, as man, to rise again and obtain eternal life through resurrection. His blood had satisfied the law and righteousness of God. By giving His lifeblood, He had overcome the power of sin and brought it to nothing. *The sting of death is sin, and the power of sin is the law* (1 Corinthians 15:56).

So death was defeated, as its sting had been removed, and the devil was also defeated, who held the power of death but now lost all right over Him and us. *Forasmuch then as the children are partakers of flesh and blood, he also himself* [Jesus] *likewise took part of the same, that through death he might destroy him that had the empire* [power] *of death, that is, the devil* (Hebrews 2:14). His blood had destroyed the power of death, the devil, and hell: *But* [God's purpose and grace] *is now made manifest by the appearing of our Saviour Jesus Christ, who has annulled death, and has brought life and incorruption to light through the gospel* (2 Timothy 1:10).

The blood of Jesus has opened the grave, and he who believes that will perceive the close connection which exists between the blood and the almighty power of God. Only through the blood does God exert His almightiness in dealing with sinful men. The resurrection power of God gives entrance into eternal life where the blood of Christ is applied. His blood has made a complete end of the power of death and hell; the effects of the blood surpass all human thought.

The Blood of Jesus Has Opened Heaven
We read in Hebrews 9:12 that *by his own blood he* [Christ] *entered in once into the sanctuary designed for eternal redemption.*

We know that in the Old Testament tabernacle God's declared presence was inside the veil. No power of man could remove that veil, and the high priest alone could enter, but only with blood, or he would lose his own life.

> *And I will dwell among the sons of Israel and shall be their God. And they shall know that I am the*

LORD their God, that brought them forth out of the land of Egypt, that I may dwell among them; I am the LORD your God. (Exodus 29:45-46)

And the LORD said unto Moses, Speak unto Aaron, thy brother, that he not enter at all times into the sanctuary inside the veil before the seat of reconciliation, which is upon the ark, that he not die; for I will appear in the cloud above the seat of reconciliation. Thus shall Aaron come into the holy place: with a young bullock as sin and a ram as a burnt offering. (Leviticus 16:2-3)

That was a picture of the power of sin in the flesh, which separates us from God. The eternal righteousness of God guarded the entrance to the most Holy Place, that no flesh might approach Him.

But now our Lord appears not in a physical temple but in the true temple. As High Priest and representative of His people, Jesus asks for an entrance into the presence of the Holy One for the sinful children of Adam. He requested that they *be with me where I am* (John 17:24). He asks that heaven may be opened for each one, even for the greatest sinner, who believes in Him. His request is granted. But how is that? It is through the blood. He entered through His own blood. The blood of Jesus has opened heaven.

For Christ is not entered into the sanctuary made with hands (which is a figure of the true), but into heaven itself, now to appear in the presence of God for us, nor yet that he should offer himself many times (as the high priest enters into the sanctuary each year with blood that is not his own); otherwise it would have been necessary for him to suffer many times since the foundation of the world; but

*now once in the consummation of the ages he has
appeared to abolish sin by the sacrifice of himself.*
(Hebrews 9:24-26)

So it is through the blood that the throne of grace remains
settled in heaven. In the midst of heaven, nearest to God the
Judge of all and to Jesus the Mediator, the Holy Spirit gives a
prominent place to the blood of sprinkling.

*Unto the city of the living God, the heavenly
Jerusalem, and to an innumerable company of
angels, to the congregation of the called out ones of
the firstborn, who are registered in the heavens and
to God the Judge of all and to the spirits of just men
made perfect and to Jesus, the mediator of the new
testament and to the blood of sprinkling, that speaks
better than that of Abel.* (Hebrews 12:22-24)

It is the constant mention of that blood that keeps heaven open
for sinners and sends streams of blessing down on earth. It is
through that blood that Jesus, as Mediator, carries on His work
as an advocate without ceasing. The throne of grace owes its
existence to the power of that blood, and we can now *come
boldly unto the throne of his grace, that we may obtain mercy
and find grace to help in time of need* (Hebrews 4:16).

Oh, the wonderful power of the blood of Christ! Just as it
has opened the gates of the grave and hell, so it has opened the
gates of heaven for us to enter through Him. The blood has an
almighty power over the kingdom of darkness and hell beneath
and over the kingdom of heaven and its glory above.

The Blood of Jesus is All Powerful in the Human Heart
Since the blood serves so powerfully with God and over Satan,
doesn't it satisfy even more powerfully with man for whose sake
it was actually shed? We may be sure of it.

The wonderful power of the blood is especially demonstrated on behalf of sinners on earth. This is emphasized in the first book of Peter: *Knowing that ye have been ransomed from your vain conversation . . . not with corruptible things like silver and gold, but with the precious blood of the Christ* (1 Peter 1:18-19).

The word *ransomed* (literally *redeemed*) has a depth of meaning. It indicates particularly deliverance from slavery by emancipation or purchase. The sinner is enslaved under the hostile power of Satan, the curse of the Law, and sin. Now it is proclaimed *ye have been ransomed* through the blood, which had paid the debt of guilt and destroyed the power of Satan, the curse, and sin.

Where this proclamation is heard and received, redemption begins in a true deliverance from a vain manner of life – from a life of sin. The word *redemption* or *ransom* includes everything God does for a sinner, beginning with the pardon of sin and giving of the Holy Spirit, which is *the earnest of our inheritance unto the redemption of the purchased possession, unto the praise of his glory* (Ephesians 1:14). It continues to the full deliverance of the body by the resurrection: *Likewise we also walk in newness of life. For if we have been planted together in him in the likeness of his death, we shall be also in the likeness of his resurrection, knowing this: that our old man is crucified with him that the body of sin might be destroyed that we should not serve sin any longer* (Romans 6:4-6).

Those to whom Peter wrote were *chosen . . . to obey and be sprinkled with the blood of Jesus, the Christ* (1 Peter 1:2). It was the proclamation about the precious blood that had touched their hearts and brought them to repentance – awakening faith in them and filling their souls with life and joy. Each believer was an illustration of the wonderful power of the blood.

Later, when Peter exhorts them to holiness, it is still the precious blood, which is his plea. *As he who has called you is*

holy, so be ye holy in all manner of conversation; for it is writ-
ten, Be ye holy; for I am holy (1 Peter 1:15-16). On that he would
fix their eyes.

For the Jew in his self-righteousness and hatred of Christ
and for the heathen in his godliness, there was only one means
of deliverance from the power of sin. It is still the one power
that accomplishes daily deliverance for sinners. How could it
be otherwise? The blood that provided so powerfully in heaven
and over hell is also all powerful in a sinner's heart.

It is impossible for us to think too highly or to expect too
much from the power of Jesus's blood.

How Can We Experience Its Effects?

This is our third question. In what conditions, under what
circumstances, can that power secure the mighty results it is
intended to produce in us?

The first answer is the same as it is everywhere in the kingdom of God – through faith.

But faith is largely dependent on knowledge. If knowledge
of what the blood can accomplish is imperfect, faith expects
little, and the more powerful effects of the blood are impossible.
Many Christians think that if they have received the assurance
of the pardon of their sins through faith in the blood, they have
a sufficient knowledge of its capability.

They have no idea that the words of God, like God Himself,
are inexhaustible; they are deprived of a wealth of meaning and
blessing that surpasses all understanding.

They do not remember that when the Holy Spirit speaks of
cleansing through the blood, such words are only the imperfect
human expressions of the effects and experiences by which
the blood, in an unspeakably glorious manner, will reveal its
heavenly life-giving power to the soul. Feeble conceptions of

its power prevent the deeper, more perfect demonstrations of its effects.

As we seek to find out what the Scripture teaches about the blood, we will see that faith in the blood can produce greater results in us than we have ever known, and in the future a ceaseless blessing may be ours.

Our faith may be strengthened by noticing what the blood has already accomplished. Heaven and hell bear witness to that. Faith will grow by exercising confidence in the superabundance of the promises of God. Let us heartily expect that as we enter more deeply into the fountain, its cleansing, quickening, life-giving power will be revealed more blessedly.

We know that in bathing we enter into the most intimate relationship with the water; we give ourselves up to its cleansing effects. The blood of Jesus is described as *an open fountain . . . against sin and against uncleanness* (Zechariah 13:1). By the power of the Holy Spirit it streams through the heavenly temple. *There is a river, the streams of which shall make glad the city of God, the sanctuary of the tents of the most High. God is in the midst of her; she shall not be moved; God shall help her, as the morning dawns* (Psalm 46:4-5). By faith I place myself in closest touch with this heavenly stream; I yield myself to it; I let it cover me and go through me. I bathe in the fountain. It cannot withhold its cleansing and strengthening power. I must in simple faith turn away from what is seen to plunge into that spiritual fountain, which represents the Savior's blood, with the assurance that it will manifest its blessed power in me.

So let us with childlike, persevering, expectant faith, open our souls to an ever-increasing experience of the wonderful power of the blood.

But there is a second reply to the question of what else is necessary for the blood to manifest its power. Scripture connects the blood most closely with the Spirit. Only where the Spirit works can the power of the blood be demonstrated.

The Spirit and the Blood

We read in 1 John that *there are three that bear witness on earth, the Spirit and the water and the blood; and these three agree in one* (1 John 5:8). The water refers to baptism unto repentance and the laying aside of sin. The blood witnesses to redemption in Christ. The Spirit is He who supplies power to the water and the blood. The Spirit and the blood are also associated in Hebrews where we read: *How much more shall the blood of the Christ, who through the eternal Spirit offered himself without spot to God, purge your conscience* (Hebrews 9:14). It was by the eternal Spirit in our Lord that His blood had its value and power.

It is always through the Spirit that the blood possesses its living power in heaven and in the hearts of men. The blood and the Spirit always bear testimony together.

Where the blood is honored in faith or preaching, the Spirit will work, and where He works, He always leads souls to the blood. The Holy Spirit could not be given until the blood was shed. The living bond between the Spirit and the blood cannot be broken.

It should be noted that if the full power of the blood is to be manifested in our souls, we must place ourselves under the teaching of the Holy Spirit. *The Comforter, which is the Holy Spirit, whom the Father will send in my name, he shall teach you all things and bring to your remembrance all the things that I have said unto you* (John 14:26).

We must firmly believe that He is in us and that He carries on His work in our hearts. Jesus prayed *that they may be one, even as we are one: I in them, and thou in me, that they may be perfect in one and that the world may know that thou hast sent me and hast loved them as thou hast loved me* (John 17:22-23).

25

We must live as those who know that the Spirit of God dwells within them as a seed of life, and He will bring to perfection the hidden, powerful effects of the blood. *But if Christ is in you, the body is truly dead because of sin, but the Spirit is alive because of righteousness. And if the Spirit of him that raised up Jesus from the dead dwells in you, he that raised up the Christ from the dead shall also quicken your mortal bodies by his Spirit that dwells in you. For all that are led by the Spirit of God, the same are sons of God* (Romans 8:10-11, 14). We must allow Him to lead us. Through the Spirit the blood will cleanse, sanctify, and unite us to God.

When the apostle desired to arouse believers to listen to God's voice with His call to holiness, *Be ye holy, for I am holy,* he reminded them that they had been redeemed by the precious blood of Christ.

Necessary Knowledge

People must know that they have been redeemed and what that redemption signifies, but above all they must know that it was *not with corruptible things like silver and gold,* things in which there was no power of life, *but with the precious blood of the Christ* (1 Peter 1:18-19).

To have a correct perception of what the preciousness of that blood was – as the power of a perfect redemption – would be the power of a new and holy life.

Beloved Christians, that statement applies to us also. We must *know* that we are redeemed by the precious blood. We must know about redemption and the blood, before we can experience its power.

We will experience more fully the blessings and benefits in proportion to how fully we understand what redemption is and what the power and preciousness of the blood are, by which redemption has been obtained.

Let us submit ourselves to the Holy Spirit to be led into a deeper knowledge of redemption through the precious blood.

Need and Desire

Two things are necessary here: first, a deeper sense of need and a desire to understand the blood better. The blood has been shed to take away sin. The power of the blood is to bring the power of sin to nothing.

However, we are too easily satisfied with the first beginnings of deliverance from sin, and what remains of that sin in us might become unbearable. May we no longer be content with the fact that we, as redeemed ones, sin against God's will in so many things.

May the desire for holiness become stronger in us. Shouldn't the thought that the blood has more power than we recognize and can do greater things than we have yet experienced cause our hearts to go out in strong desire? If there were more desire for deliverance from sin, for holiness and intimate friendship with a holy God, we would have the first thing that is necessary to be led further into the knowledge of what the blood can do.

Expectation

The second thing will follow. Desire must become expectation. As we search the Word in faith to discern what the blood has accomplished, it must be a settled matter with us that the blood can demonstrate its full power in us also. No sense of unworthiness, ignorance, or helplessness should cause us to doubt. The blood works in the surrendered soul with a ceaseless power of life.

So, surrender yourself to God the Holy Spirit. Fix the eyes of your heart on the blood. Open your whole inner being to its power. The blood on which the throne of grace in heaven is founded can make your heart the temple and throne of God.

Find your shelter under the sprinkling of the blood and ask the Lamb of God Himself to make the blood effective in you. You will surely discover that there is nothing to compare with the wonder-working power of the blood of Jesus.

Chapter 3

Reconciliation Through the Blood

Being justified freely by his grace through the redemption that is in Jesus, the Christ, whom God purposed for reconciliation through faith in his blood. (Romans 3:24-25)

A s we have seen, several distinct blessings have been acquired for us by the power of the blood of Jesus, which are all included in the one word *redemption*. Among these blessings, reconciliation takes first place.[2] *God purposed for reconciliation through faith in his blood.* In our Lord's work of redemption, reconciliation naturally comes first. It also stands first among the needs of the sinner who desires to have a share in redemption. Through reconciliation, a participation in the other blessings of redemption is possible.

It is of great importance also that the believer who has been reconciled should obtain a deeper and more spiritual understanding of its meaning and blessedness. If the power of the blood in redemption is rooted in reconciliation, then a more complete knowledge of reconciliation is the surest way to obtain

---

2   To reconcile: To restore to fellowship or harmony; to repair or recompense.

a greater experience of the power of the blood. The heart that is surrendered to the teaching of the Holy Spirit will surely learn what reconciliation means. May our hearts be opened wide to receive it.

To understand what reconciliation by the blood means, let us consider the following points:

1. Sin has made reconciliation necessary.

2. God's holiness foreordained reconciliation.

3. The blood of Jesus obtained reconciliation.

4. The pardon resulted from reconciliation.

Sin Has Made Reconciliation Necessary

In all the work of Christ, and above all in reconciliation, God's objective is the removal and destruction of sin. Knowledge of sin is necessary for the knowledge of reconciliation.

We want to understand what there is in sin that needs reconciling or repairing and how reconciliation renders sin powerless. Then faith will have something to take hold of, and the experience of that blessing is made possible.

Sin has had a twofold effect. It has had an effect on God, as well as on man. We usually emphasize its effect on man. But the effect it has exercised on God is more terrible and serious. Because of its effect on God, that sin has power over us. God, as Lord of all, could not overlook sin. His unalterable law declares that sin will bring forth sorrow and death. When man fell into sin, by the law of God, he was brought under the power of sin. So, the law of God required that redemption must begin, for if sin is powerless against God, and the law of God gives sin no authority over us, then its power is destroyed. The knowledge that sin is speechless before God assures us that it no longer has authority over us.

What then was the effect of sin upon God? In His divine nature, He remains unchanged and unchangeable, but in His relationship and acceptance toward man, an entire change took place. Sin is disobedience, a contempt of the authority of God; it seeks to rob God of His honor as God and Lord. Sin is determined opposition to a holy God. It not only can, but must, awaken His wrath.

While it was God's desire to continue in love and friendship with man, sin has compelled Him to become an opponent. Although the love of God toward man remains unchanged, sin made it impossible for Him to admit man into fellowship with Himself. It has compelled Him to pour out His wrath and punishment instead of His love upon man. The change that sin caused in God's relationship to man is horrible. But *God purposed for reconciliation through faith in his blood for the manifestation of his righteousness, for the remission of sins that are past* (Romans 3:25).

Man is guilty before God. Guilt involves debt. We know what debt is. It is something that one person can demand from another, a claim which must be met and settled.

When sin is committed, its after-effects may or may not be noticed, but its guilt always remains. The sinner is guilty. God cannot disregard His own demand that sin must be punished; His glory, which has been dishonored, must be upheld. As long as the debt is not paid or the guilt abolished, it is impossible for a holy God to allow the sinner to come into His presence.

We often think that the great question for us is how we can be delivered from the indwelling power of sin, but that is a question of less importance than how can we be delivered from the guilt which is heaped up before God? Can the guilt of sin be removed? Can the effect of sin upon God in awakening His wrath be removed? Can sin be blotted out before God? If these things can be done, the power of sin will be broken in us. Only through reconciliation can the guilt of sin be removed.

The word translated *reconciliation* actually means "to cover." Even heathen people had an understanding of this. But in Israel God revealed a reconciliation that could not only cover but could also remove the guilt of sin, so the original relationship between God and man can be entirely restored. This is what true reconciliation must do. It must remove the guilt of sin, the effect of sin on God, so man can draw near to God in the blessed assurance that there is no longer the least guilt resting on him to keep him away from God.

God's Holiness Foreordained Reconciliation

God's holiness must also be considered if we are to understand reconciliation correctly. It is His infinite, glorious perfection, which always leads Him to desire what is good in others as well as in Himself. He applies and works out that good and hates and condemns all that is opposed to the good.

In His holiness, both the love and wrath of God are united – His love, which gives itself, and His wrath, which casts out and consumes what is evil according to the divine law of righteousness.

As the Holy One, God ordained reconciliation in Israel and took up His abode on the mercy seat.

As the Holy One in expectation of New Testament times, He often said, I am *thy Redeemer, the Holy One of Israel* (Isaiah 48:17).

As the Holy One, God worked out His law of reconciliation in Christ.

The wonder of this law is that both the holy love and the holy wrath of God find satisfaction in it. Apparently, they were in irreconcilable strife with one another. The holy love was unwilling to let man go. *Not because we had loved God, but because he loved us and has sent his Son to be the reconciliation for our sins* (1 John 4:10). In spite of his sin, holy love could not give him up; man had to be redeemed. The holy wrath could not surrender its demands. The law had been despised; God had been dishonored. God's righteousness had to be upheld. The sinner could not be released as long as the law was not satisfied. The terrible effect of sin in heaven on God had to be corrected; the guilt of sin had to be removed. Otherwise, the sinner could not be delivered. The only solution possible was reconciliation. We have seen that *reconciliation* means "covering." It means that something else has taken the place where sin was established, so that sin can no longer be seen by God.

But because God is the Holy One and His eyes are as a flame of fire, whatever covered sin had to be of such a nature that it counteracted the evil that sin had done. It had to blot out sin so it was really destroyed and could not be seen.

Reconciliation for sin can take place only by satisfaction. Satisfaction is reconciliation, and it originates through a substitute. In this way sin can be punished, and the sinner saved. God's holiness also would be glorified, and its demands met, as well as the demand of God's love in the redemption of the sinner and the demand of His righteousness in the maintenance of the glory of God and His law.

We know how this was accomplished in the Old Testament laws of the offerings. *The priest shall reconcile him before the LORD, and he shall have forgiveness for any of all the things in which he is guilty* (Leviticus 6:7). A clean beast took the place of a guilty man. By confession, his sin was laid on the head of the victim, which bore the punishment by surrendering its life unto death. Then the blood, representing a clean life that is free from guilt, can be brought into God's presence; the blood or life of the beast has borne the punishment in place of the sinner. That blood made reconciliation and covered the sinner and his sin, because it had taken the sinner's place and atoned for his sin.

There was reconciliation through the blood, but it was not a reality. *Every priest stands daily ministering and offering many times the same sacrifices, which can never take away sins* (Hebrews 10:11). The blood of cattle or of goats could never take away sin; it was only a shadow or picture of the real reconciliation.

Blood of a different character was necessary for an effectual covering of guilt. *But Christ being now come, high priest of the good things to come, by a greater and more perfect tabernacle, . . . neither by the blood of goats and calves, but by his own blood he entered in once into the sanctuary designed for eternal redemption* (Hebrews 9:11-12). According to the law of the Holy God, nothing less than the blood of God's own Son could bring about reconciliation. Righteousness demanded it; love offered it. *Being justified freely by his grace through the redemption that is in Jesus, the Christ, whom God purposed for reconciliation through faith in his blood* (Romans 3:24-25).

The Blood of Jesus Obtained Reconciliation

Reconciliation must be the satisfaction of the demands of God's holy law. The Lord Jesus accomplished that; by a willing and perfect obedience, He fulfilled the law under which He had placed Himself. In the same spirit of complete surrender to the will of the Father, He bore the curse, which the law had pronounced against sin. *He himself bore our sins in his own body on the tree, that we, being dead to sins, should live unto righteousness; by whose wound ye were healed* (1 Peter 2:24). He rendered in fullest measure of obedience or punishment all that the law of God could ever ask or desire. The law was perfectly satisfied by Him.

But how can His fulfilling of the demands of the law be reconciliation for the sins of others? Because both in creation and in the covenant of grace that the Father had made with Him, He was recognized as the head of the human race. Because of this, He was able to become a second Adam by becoming flesh. *For he has made him to be sin for us, who knew no sin, that we might be made the righteousness of God in him* (2 Corinthians 5:21). When He, the Word, became flesh, He placed Himself in a real fellowship with our flesh, which was under the power of sin; He assumed the responsibility for all that sin had done in the flesh against God. His obedience and perfection were not merely that of one man among others, but that of Him who had placed Himself in fellowship with all other men and had taken their sin upon Himself.

As Head of mankind through creation and as their representative in the covenant, Jesus became their guarantee. He perfectly satisfied the demands of the law by the shedding of His blood; this was the reconciliation, the covering of our sin.

Above all, we must never forget that Jesus was God with a divine power to unite Himself with His creatures and to take them up into Himself. It imparted on His sufferings a virtue of infinite holiness and power and made the merit of His blood-shedding more than sufficient to deal with all the guilt of human sin. His blood became a real reconciliation, a perfect covering of sin, so the holiness of God no longer sees the sin. In truth, it has been blotted out. The blood of Jesus, God's Son, has acquired a real, perfect, and eternal reconciliation.

What does that mean?

We have spoken of the horrible effect of sin on God and the terrible change that took place in heaven through sin. Instead of favor, friendship, blessing, and the life of God from heaven, man had nothing to look for except wrath, death, and condemnation. Man could think of God only with fear and terror, without hope and without love. Sin never ceased to call for vengeance; guilt had to be dealt with in full.

But the blood of Jesus, God's Son, has been shed. Atonement for sin has been made. Peace is restored. A change has taken place again as real and widespread as that which sin had brought about. For those who receive the reconciliation, sin has been brought to nothing. The wrath of God turns around and hides itself in the depth of divine love.

The righteousness of God no longer terrifies man. It is written to us that *to those that believe in him that raised up Jesus our Lord from the dead, who was delivered for our offenses and was raised again for our justification. Justified therefore by faith, we have peace with God through our Lord Jesus, the Christ* (Romans 4:24-25; 5:1).

God's righteousness meets man as a friend with an offer of complete justification. God's countenance beams with pleasure and approval as the penitent sinner draws near to Him, and He invites him into intimate fellowship. He opens a treasure of blessing, and there is nothing now that can separate him from God.

> *Nevertheless, in all these things we are more than conquerors through him that loved us. Therefore I am certain that neither death nor life nor angels nor principalities nor powers nor things present nor things to come nor height nor depth nor any creature shall be able to separate us from the charity [love] of God, which is in Christ, Jesus our Lord.* (Romans 8:37-39)

The reconciliation through the blood of Jesus has covered man's sins; they no longer appear in God's sight. He no longer charges him for sin. Reconciliation has worked out a perfect and eternal redemption.

Who can tell the worth of that precious blood? It is no wonder that mention will be made forever of that blood in the song of the redeemed and through all eternity; as long as heaven lasts, the praise of the blood will resound: *Thou wast slain and hast redeemed us unto God by thy blood* (Revelation 5:9).

But here is the wonder: that the redeemed on earth do not join in that song more heartily and that they are not abounding in praise for the reconciliation that the power of the blood has accomplished.

The Pardon Resulted from Reconciliation

The blood has made reconciliation for sin and covered it, and as a result of this, a wonderful change has taken place in the heavenly realms. But all this will avail us nothing unless we obtain a personal share in it. Only in the pardon of sin can this take place.

God has offered a perfect acquittal from all our sin and guilt. Because reconciliation has been made for sin, we can now be reconciled, or restored, to Him. *God was in Christ, reconciling the world unto himself, not imputing their trespasses unto them* (2 Corinthians 5:19). Following this is the invitation to *be ye reconciled to God* (2 Corinthians 5:20). Whoever *receives* reconciliation for sin *is* reconciled to God. He knows that all his sins are forgiven.

The Scriptures use various illustrations to emphasize the extent of forgiveness and to convince the fearful heart of the sinner that the blood has really taken his sin away. *I have undone, as a cloud, thy rebellions, and thy sins, as a mist* (Isaiah 44:22). *Thou hast cast all my sins behind thy back* (Isaiah 38:17). *He.. . will cast all our sins into the depths of the sea* (Micah 7:19). *The iniquity of Israel shall be sought for, and there shall be none; and the sins of Judah, and they shall not be found: for I will pardon those whom I shall have left* (Jeremiah 50:20).

This is what the New Testament calls justification. It is thus named in Romans 3:23-26: *For all have sinned . . . being justified freely* [for nothing] *by his grace through the redemption that is in Jesus, the Christ, whom God purposed for reconciliation through faith in his blood for the manifestation of his righteousness, . . . that he only be the just one and the justifier of him that is of the faith of Jesus.*

So perfect is the reconciliation and so completely has sin been covered and blotted out that he who believes in Christ is looked upon and treated by God as entirely righteous. The acquittal that man has received from God is so complete that there is nothing, absolutely nothing, to prevent him from approaching God with the utmost freedom.

Nothing is necessary for the enjoyment of this blessedness except faith in the blood. The blood alone has done everything.

The penitent sinner who turns from his sin to God needs only faith in that blood, that is, faith in the power of the blood that it has truly atoned for sin and that it has atoned for him. Through that faith, he knows that he is more completely reconciled to God, and that there is now nothing to hinder God from pouring out on him the fullness of His love and blessing.

If man looks toward heaven, which formerly was covered with clouds, black with God's wrath and a coming judgment, that cloud will no longer to be seen; everything is bright in the light of God's face and God's love. Faith in the blood produces in his heart the same wonder-working power that it exercised in heaven. Through faith in the blood, he becomes a partaker of all the blessings that the blood has obtained for him from God.

Fellow believers, pray earnestly that the Holy Spirit may reveal to you the glory of this reconciliation, and the pardon of your sins may be yours through the blood of Jesus. Pray for enlightened hearts to see how completely the accusing and condemning power of your sin has been removed and how God in the fullness of His love and good pleasure has turned toward you. Open your hearts to the Holy Spirit that He may reveal in you the glorious effects which the blood has had in heaven. God has set Jesus Christ Himself as a reconciliation through faith in His blood. He is the reconciliation for our sins. Rely on Him as having already covered your sin before God. Set Him between yourselves and your sins, and you will experience how complete the redemption is, which He has accomplished, and how powerful the reconciliation is through faith in His blood.

Then through the living Christ, the powerful effects that the blood has exercised in heaven will increasingly be produced in your hearts, and you will know what it means to walk by the Spirit's grace in the full light and enjoyment of forgiveness.

And you who have not yet obtained forgiveness of your sins, doesn't this word come to you as an urgent call to faith in His blood? Will you never allow yourselves to be moved by what God has done for you as sinners? *In this does the charity [love] consist, not because we had loved God, but because he loved us and has sent his Son to be the reconciliation for our sins* (1 John 4:10).

The precious, divine blood has been shed; reconciliation is complete, and the message comes to you: *Be ye reconciled to God* (2 Corinthians 5:20).

If you repent of your sins and desire to be delivered from sin's power and bondage, exercise faith in the blood. Open your heart to the influence of the word that God has sent to be spoken unto you. Open your heart to the message that the blood can deliver you – yes, even you, this moment. Only believe it. Say, "that blood is also for me." If you come as a guilty, lost sinner, longing for pardon, you may rest assured that the blood that has already made a perfect reconciliation covers *your* sin and restores *you* immediately to the favor and love of God.

So I pray you, exercise faith in the blood. This moment bow down before God and tell Him that you do believe in the power of the blood for your own soul. Having said that, stand by it, cling to it. Through faith in His blood, Jesus Christ will be the reconciliation for your sins also. *For it pleased the Father that in him should all fullness dwell and by him to reconcile all things unto himself, having made peace through the blood of his cross* (Colossians 1:19-20).

Chapter 4

Cleansing Through the Blood

*If we walk in the light, as he is in the light, we have
communion with him in the midst of us, and the
blood of Jesus Christ, his Son cleanses us from all
sin.* (1 John 1:7)

W e have already seen that the most important effect of
the blood is reconciliation for sin. The fruit of knowledge about and faith in reconciliation is the pardon of sin.
Pardon is just a declaration of what has already taken place in
heaven on the sinner's behalf and his hearty acceptance of it.

This first effect of the blood is not the only one. The blood
exerts a further power in proportion to how the soul, through
faith, yields itself to the Spirit of God. The soul can understand
and enjoy the full power of reconciliation, as the blood imparts
other blessings, which Scripture attributes to it.

One of the first results of reconciliation is cleansing from
sin. We need to see what God's Word says about this. Cleansing
is often spoken about among us as if it were no more than the
pardon of sins or the cleansing from guilt. This, however, is
not so. Scripture does not speak of being *cleansed from guilt.*

Cleansing from sin means deliverance from the pollution, not from the guilt of sin. The guilt of sin concerns our relationship to God and our responsibility to correct our errors or bear the punishment of them. The pollution of sin, on the other hand, is the sense of defilement and impurity which sin brings to our inner being, and this is what cleansing deals with.

Cleansing is of the greatest importance for every believer who desires to enjoy the full salvation that God has provided for him and to understand correctly what the Scriptures teach about it.

Let us consider:

1. What the word *cleansing* means in the Old Testament.

2. What the word *blessing* indicates in the New Testament.

3. How we may experience the full enjoyment of this blessing.

Cleansing in the Old Testament

In the service of God as ordained by the hand of Moses for Israel, two ceremonies had to be observed by God's people before approaching Him. These were the offerings or sacrifices and the cleansings or purifications. Both were to be observed but in different manners. Both were intended to remind man of how sinful he was and how unfit to draw near to a holy God. Both were to typify the redemption by which the Lord Jesus Christ would restore man's fellowship with God. As a rule, it is only the offerings which are regarded as typical of redemption through Christ. The epistle to the Hebrews, however, emphatically mentions the cleansings as figures for the time being in

foods and drinks and different washings and carnal ordinances,
imposed on them until the time of correction (Hebrews 9:10).

If we can imagine the life of an Israelite, we shall understand that the consciousness of sin and the need for redemption were awakened as much by the cleansings as by the offerings. We must also learn from them what the power of the blood of Jesus actually is.

We may take one of the more important examples of cleansing as an illustration. If anyone was in a hut or house where a dead body lay, or if he had even touched a dead body or bones, he was unclean for seven days. Death, as the punishment for sin, made everyone who came into association with it unclean. Cleansing was accomplished by using the ashes of a young heifer, which had been burned as described in Numbers:

> *And a man that is clean shall gather up the ashes*
> *of the heifer and lay them up outside the camp in*
> *a clean place, and it shall be kept for the congrega-*
> *tion of the sons of Israel for the water of separa-*
> *tion; it is sin. And he that gathers the ashes of the*
> *heifer shall wash his clothes and be unclean until*
> *the evening; . . . Whoever touches the dead body of*
> *anyone that is dead and does not remove the sin*
> *has defiled the tabernacle of the LORD; . . . And for*
> *the unclean person they shall take of the dust of the*
> *heifer that was burnt as sin and put living water*
> *over it in a vessel; and a clean person shall take*
> *hyssop and dip it in the water and sprinkle it upon*
> *the tent and upon all the stuff and upon the persons*
> *that were there and upon the one that touched the*
> *bone or the one slain or the one dead or the grave.*
> (Numbers 19:9-10, 13, 17-18)

These ashes, mixed with water, were sprinkled by means of a

bunch of hyssop on the one who was unclean; he then had to bathe himself in water to be once more ceremonially clean.

The words *unclean, cleansing,* and *clean* were used in reference to the healing of leprosy, a disease that might be described as a living death. In Leviticus 13 and 14, we also see that he who was to be cleansed had to first be sprinkled with water, in which the blood of a sacrificially offered bird had been mixed. Then he had to bathe in water. Seven days later he was again sprinkled with sacrificial blood.

A close consideration of the laws of cleansing will teach us that the difference between the cleansings and the offerings was twofold. First, the offering had definite reference to the transgression for which reconciliation had to be made. Cleansing had more to do with conditions which were not sinful in themselves but were the result of sin, and therefore had to be acknowledged by God's holy people as defiling. Secondly, in the case of the offering, nothing was done to the offeror himself. He saw the blood sprinkled on the altar or carried into the Holy Place; he had to believe that this obtained reconciliation before God. But nothing was done to himself. In cleansing, on the other hand, what happened to the person was the chief thing. Defilement was something that either through internal disease or outward touch had come upon the man, so the washing or sprinkling with water must take place on himself as ordained by God.

Cleansing was something that he could feel and experience. It brought about a change not only in his relationship to God but also in his own condition. In the offering, something was done *for* him; with cleansing, something was done *in* him. The offering had respect to his guilt. The cleansing dealt with the pollution of sin.

The same meaning of the words *clean* and *cleansing* is found elsewhere in the Old Testament. David prays in Psalm 51, *cleanse me from my sin. . . . Remove the sin in me with hyssop, and I shall be clean* (Psalm 51:2, 7). The word used by David here is that which is used most frequently for the cleansing of anyone who had touched a dead body. Hyssop also was used in such cases. David prayed for more than pardon. He confessed that he had been *shapen in iniquity*, that his nature was sinful (Psalm 51:5 KJV). He prayed that he might be made pure within. *Cleanse me from my sin* was his prayer. He uses the same word later when he prays, *Create in me a clean heart, O God* (Psalm 51:10). Cleansing is more than pardon.

In the same manner this word is used by Ezekiel and refers to an inner condition which must be changed. The Lord, *because I have cleansed thee, and thou didst not cleanse thyself* (Ezekiel 24:13). Later, speaking of the new covenant, He says, *And I will sprinkle clean water upon you, and ye shall be cleansed from all your filthiness, and from all your idols will I cleanse you* (Ezekiel 36:25).

Malachi says the same thing, connecting it with fire: *he shall sit to refine and to purify the silver: he shall purify* [cleanse] *the sons of Levi* (Malachi 3:3).

Cleansing by water, by blood, and by fire are all typical of the cleansing which would take place under the new covenant – an inner cleansing and deliverance from the stain of sin.

Blessing in the New Testament

Mention is often made in the New Testament of a clean or pure heart. Our Lord said, *Blessed are the pure in heart* (Matthew 5:8). Paul speaks of *charity* [love] *out of a pure heart* (1 Timothy 1:5). He speaks also of a *good conscience*.

Peter exhorts his readers to *love one another with a pure heart fervently* (1 Peter 1:22). The word *cleansing* is also used.

We read of those who are described as God's people *purifying* [cleansing] *their hearts by faith* (Acts 15:9). The purpose of the Lord Jesus concerning those who were His was to *purify* [cleanse] *unto himself a people of his own* (Titus 2:14).

As regards ourselves we read: *Let us cleanse ourselves from all filthiness of the flesh and spirit* (2 Corinthians 7:1).

All these Scriptures teach us that cleansing is an inward condition produced in the heart as a result of pardon.

We are told in 1 John 1:7 that *the blood of Jesus Christ, his Son cleanses us from all sin.* The word *cleanses* does not refer to the grace of pardon received at conversion but to the effect of grace in God's children who walk in the light. We read also in verse 7 that *if we walk in the light, as he is in the light, . . . the blood of Jesus Christ, his Son cleanses us from all sin.* What follows in verse 9 shows that something more than pardon is indicated: *He is faithful and just to forgive us our sins and to cleanse us from all unrighteousness.* Cleansing is something that comes after pardon and is the result of it by the inward and experiential reception of the power of the blood of Jesus in the heart of the believer.

This takes place according to the Word by the purifying of the conscience. *How much more shall the blood of Christ, . . . purge your conscience from the works of death to serve the living God?* (Hebrews 9:14). The earlier mention of sprinkling the ashes of a heifer on the unclean serves as an example of a personal experience of the precious blood of Christ. Conscience is not only a judge to give sentence on our actions, but it is also the inward voice, which bears witness to our relationship with God. When it is cleansed by the blood, it bears witness that we are well pleasing to God.

It is written in Hebrews, *those that sacrifice, once purged, would have no more conscience of sins* (Hebrews 10:2). Through the Spirit we receive an inward experience that the blood has delivered us from the guilt and power of sin, so in our regenerated nature, we have escaped entirely from sin's dominion.

Sin still dwells in our flesh, with its temptations, but it has no power to rule. The conscience is cleansed; there is no need for the least bit of separation between God and us. We look up to Him in the full power of redemption. The conscience, which is cleansed by the blood, bears witness to nothing less than a complete redemption – the fullness of God's good pleasure.

And if the conscience is cleansed, so is the heart, of which the conscience is the center. We read of having the heart *purified from an evil conscience* (Hebrews 10:22). Not only must the conscience be cleansed, but the heart also must be cleansed, including the understanding and the will with all our thoughts and desires. The death and resurrection of Christ are ceaselessly effective. By this power of His death and resurrection, sinful lusts and dispositions are slain.

The blood of Jesus Christ, his Son cleanses us from all sin – from original as well as from actual sin. The blood exercises its spiritual, heavenly power in the soul, and the believer, in whose life the blood is effective, experiences his old nature being hindered from manifesting its power. Through the blood, lusts and desires are subdued and slain, and everything is so cleansed that the Spirit can bring forth His glorious fruit. In case of the least stumbling, the soul finds immediate cleansing and restoration. Even unconscious sins are rendered powerless through its effectiveness.

We have noted a difference between the guilt and the pollution of sin. This is important for a clear understanding of the matter, but in actual life, we must remember that they are not distinguished. Through the blood, God deals with sin as a whole. Every true operation of the blood demonstrates its power simultaneously over the guilt and the pollution of sin. Reconciliation and cleansing always go together, and the blood is always available.

Many seem to think that the blood is there so that if we sin again, we can turn to it again to be cleansed. But this is not so. Just as a fountain always flows and always purifies what is placed in it, so it is with this Fountain, opened for sin and uncleanness. *In that time there shall be an open fountain for the house of David and for the inhabitants of Jerusalem against sin and against uncleanness* (Zechariah 13:1). The eternal power of life of the eternal Spirit works through the blood. Through Him the heart can always abide under the flow and cleansing of the blood.

In the Old Testament, cleansing was necessary for each sin. In the New Testament, cleansing depends on Him who lives forever to intercede. When faith sees and desires and lays hold of this fact, the heart can abide every moment under the protecting and cleansing power of the blood.

Enjoyment of the Blessing

Everyone who obtains a share in the atoning merit of the blood of Christ through faith has a share also in its cleansing effectiveness. But the experience of its power to cleanse is sadly imperfect. It is therefore of great importance to understand what the conditions are for the full enjoyment of this glorious blessing.

First of all, knowledge is necessary. Many think that pardon of sin is all that we receive through the blood. They ask for and so obtain nothing more.

But we are blessed when we begin to see that the Holy Spirit of God has a special purpose in using different words in Scripture about the effects of the blood. Then we inquire about their special meaning. Let everyone who longs to know what the Lord desires to teach us by this one word compare all the places in Scripture where the word *cleansing* is used. He will soon understand that there is more promised to the believer than the removal of guilt. He will begin to understand that cleansing can provide a blessed inward resource. Knowledge of this fact is the first condition of experiencing it.

Secondly, there must be desire. Our Christianity is too often inclined to postpone the experience of what our Lord intended for our earthly life: *Blessed are the pure in heart, for they shall see God* (Matthew 5:8).

Purity of heart is a characteristic of every child of God and the necessary condition of fellowship with Him and enjoyment of His salvation. But man has too little inner longing to be in all things, at all times, well pleasing to the Lord. Sin and the stain of sin trouble us too little.

God's Word comes to us with the promise of blessing, which ought to awaken all our desires. Believe that the blood of Jesus cleanses from all sin. If you learn how to yield yourself correctly, it can do great things in you. Shouldn't you desire to experience its glorious cleansing effectiveness every hour? Shouldn't you yearn to be preserved from the many stains for which your conscience is accusing you? May your desires be awakened to long for this blessing. Put God to the test to work out in you what He as the Faithful One has promised – cleansing from all unrighteousness.

The third condition is a willingness to separate yourself from everything that is unclean. Through sin, everything in our nature and in the world is defiled. Cleansing cannot take place where there is not an entire separation from and giving up of everything unclean. *Do not touch the unclean thing* is God's command to His chosen ones (2 Corinthians 6:17). We must recognize that all the things surrounding us are unclean.

My friends, my possessions, my spirit must all be surrendered that I may be cleansed in each relationship by the precious blood and that all the activities of my spirit, soul, and being may experience a thorough cleansing.

He who will keep back anything cannot obtain the full

blessing. He who is willing to pay the full price to have his whole being baptized by the blood is on the way to understanding the blood of Jesus cleanses from all sin.

The last condition is exercising faith in the power of the blood. The blood always retains its power and effectiveness, but our unbelief closes our hearts and hinders its potential. Faith is simply the removal of that hindrance, the setting open of our hearts, for the divine power by which the living Lord will apply His blood. Yes, let us believe that there is cleansing through the blood.

You have perhaps seen a spring in the midst of a patch of grass. Dust is constantly falling over the grass that grows by the side of the road, but there is no sign of dust where the water from the spring falls in a refreshing and cleansing spray; everything is green and fresh. So the precious blood of Christ carries on its blessed work without ceasing in the soul of the believer. To the one who by faith commits himself to the Lord and believes that this can and will take place, it will be given to him.

The heavenly, spiritual effect of the blood can be experienced every moment. Its power is such that we can always abide in the fountain, always dwell in the wounds of my Lord.

I entreat you to come and prove how the blood of Jesus can cleanse your heart from all sin. You know with what joy a weary traveler would bathe in a fresh stream, plunging into the water to experience its cooling, cleansing, and strengthening effect. Lift up your eyes and see by faith how ceaselessly a stream flows from heaven above to earth beneath. Place yourself in this stream and believe that the words *the blood of Jesus cleanses from all sin* have a divine meaning – deeper and wider than you have ever imagined. Believe that the Lord Jesus Himself is the One who will cleanse you in His blood and fulfill His promise of power in you. Realize the cleansing from sin by His blood as a blessing in the daily enjoyment of which you can confidently abide.

Chapter 5

Sanctification Through the Blood

*Therefore, Jesus also, that he might sanctify the
people with his own blood, suffered outside the gate.*
(Hebrews 13:12)

Cleansing through the blood was the subject of our last
chapter. Sanctification through the blood must now
occupy our attention. To a superficial observer it might seem
that there is little difference between cleansing and sanctification. The two words seem to mean about the same thing, but
the difference is great and important. Cleansing chiefly deals
with the old life and the stain of sin, which must be removed.
Sanctification concerns the new life and the characteristics
imparted by God. Sanctification involves union with God and
the peculiar fullness of blessing purchased by the blood.

The distinction between these two fundamentals is clearly
marked in Scripture. Paul reminds us that *Christ also loved the
congregation* [church] *and gave himself for her, that he might
sanctify and cleanse her in the washing of water by the word*
(Ephesians 5:25-26). Having first cleansed it, He then sanctifies it. Writing to Timothy he says, *If a man, therefore, purges*

himself from these things, he shall be a vessel unto honour, sanctified, and profitable for the master's use, and prepared unto every good work (2 Timothy 2:21). Sanctification is a blessing which follows after and surpasses cleansing.

This distinction is also illustrated by the ordinances connected with the consecration of the priests compared with those of the Levites. In the case of the latter, who took a lower position than the priests in the service of the sanctuary, sanctification is not mentioned, but the word *cleanse* is used four times (Numbers 8).

In the consecration of the priests, however, the word *sanctify* is used often, for the priests stood in a closer relationship to God than the Levites (Exodus 29; Leviticus 8).

This record emphasizes the close connection between the sacrificial blood and sanctification. In the case of the consecration of the Levites, reconciliation for sin was made, and they were sprinkled with the water of purification for cleansing, but they were not sprinkled with blood. But blood had to be sprinkled on the priests. They were sanctified by a more personal and intimate application of the blood.

All this foreshadowed the sanctification through the blood of Jesus, and this is what we now seek to understand, so we may obtain a share in it.

Let us then consider:

1. What sanctification is.

2. How sanctification is related to the sufferings of Christ.

3. How sanctification is obtained.

What Sanctification Is

To understand what the sanctification of the redeemed is, we must first learn what the holiness of God is. He alone is the Holy One. Holiness in the creature can only be received from Him. God's holiness is often spoken of as it relates to His hatred of and hostility to sin, but this does not explain what holiness actually is. It is merely a negative statement – that God's holiness cannot bear sin.

Holiness is that attribute of God whereby He always *is*, *wills*, and *does* what is supremely good, and He desires what is supremely good in His creatures and gives it to them.

God is called *the Holy One* in Scripture, not only because He punishes sin, but also because He is the Redeemer of His people. The prophet Isaiah captured the essence of who God is: *Thus saith the LORD, your redeemer, the Holy one of Israel; . . . I am the LORD, your Holy One, the creator of Israel, your King* (Isaiah 43:14-15). His holiness is what wills what is good for all; it moved Him to redeem sinners. Both the wrath of God that punishes sin and the love of God that redeems the sinner spring from the same source – His holiness. Holiness is the perfection of God's nature.

Holiness in man is a disposition in entire agreement with that of God, which chooses in all things to will as God wills. As it is written, *As he who has called you is holy, so be ye holy* (1 Peter 1:15). Holiness in us is nothing more than oneness with God. The sanctification of God's people is effected by their intimacy with the holiness of God. There is no other way of obtaining sanctification except by the Holy God giving what He alone possesses. He alone is the Holy One. He is the Lord who sanctifies.

By the different meanings which Scripture attaches to the words *sanctification* and *to sanctify*, a relationship that we are brought into with God is emphasized.

The first and simplest meaning of the word *sanctification* is "separation." That which is taken out of its surroundings by

God's command and set aside or separated as His own possession and for His service is holy. This does not mean separation from sin only but also from all that is in the world, even from what may be permissible. In this way God sanctified the seventh day. The other days were not unclean, for *God saw every thing that he had made, and, behold, it was very good* (Genesis 1:31). But the seventh day alone was holy, for God had taken possession of it by His own special act.

In the same way, God had separated Israel from other nations, and in Israel He had separated the priests to be holy unto Him. This separation unto sanctification is always God's own work, so the electing grace of God is often closely connected with sanctification. *Ye must, therefore, be holy unto me, for I the LORD am holy and have separated you from the other peoples, that ye should be mine* (Leviticus 20:26). *The man whom the LORD chooses, he shall be holy* (Numbers 16:7). *Thou art a holy people unto the LORD thy God; the LORD thy God has chosen thee* (Deuteronomy 7:6). God cannot take part with other lords. He must be the sole possessor and ruler of those to whom He reveals and imparts His holiness.

But this separation is not the only thing included in the word *sanctification*. When separated, man stands before God, not different from a lifeless object that has been sanctified to the service of God. If the separation is to be of value, something more must take place. Man must surrender himself willingly and heartily to this separation. Sanctification includes personal consecration to the Lord to be His.

Sanctification can become ours only when it sends its roots into and takes up its abode in the depths of our personal life – in our will and in our love. God sanctifies no man against his will; therefore, the personal, hearty surrender to God is an indispensable part of this process.

It is for this reason that the Scriptures not only speak of God sanctifying us, but they also say that we must sanctify ourselves.

But even by consecration, true sanctification is not yet complete. Separation and consecration are only the preparation for the glorious work that God will do as He imparts His own holiness to the soul. Being made *participants of the divine nature* is the blessing which is promised to believers through sanctification (2 Peter 1:4). *That we might be partakers of his holiness* – that is God's desire for those whom He separates for Himself (Hebrews 12:10). But this impartation of His holiness is not a gift of something that is apart from God Himself; no, it is in personal fellowship with Him and partaking of His divine life that sanctification can be obtained.

As the Holy One, God dwelt among the people of Israel to sanctify his people. He told them, *I will dwell among the sons of Israel and shall be their God. And they shall know that I am the LORD their God, that brought them forth out of the land of Egypt, that I may dwell among them; I am the LORD your God* (Exodus 29:45-46). As the Holy One, He dwells in us. The presence of God alone can sanctify. Our portion is so sure that Scripture does not shrink from speaking of God dwelling in our hearts that we may be *filled with all the fullness of God* (Ephesians 3:19). True sanctification is fellowship with God and His dwelling in us. So it was necessary that God in Christ should take up His abode in the flesh, and that the Holy Spirit should come to dwell in us. This is what sanctification means.

How Sanctification Is Related to the Sufferings of Christ

The connection is plainly stated in Hebrews: *Jesus also, that he might sanctify his people with his own blood, suffered outside the gate* (Hebrews 13:12). In the wisdom of God, the highest destiny of man is a participation in His holiness. Therefore, this was the central objective of the coming of our Lord Jesus to earth – above His sufferings and death. It was *that he might sanctify his people* and *that we should be holy and without blemish* (Ephesians 1:4).

How the sufferings of Christ accomplished this and became our sanctification is made plain to us by the words which He spoke to His Father when He was about to become a sacrifice. *For their sakes I sanctify myself, that they also might be sanctified in the truth* (John 17:19). It was because His sufferings and death were a sanctification of Himself that they can become sanctification for us.

What does that mean? Jesus was the Holy One of God, The Son *whom the Father has sanctified and sent into the world*; must He sanctify Himself? (John 10:36). He had to do it; it was essential.

The sanctification that He possessed was not beyond the reach of temptation. In His temptation He had to maintain it and show how perfectly His will was surrendered to the holiness of God. We have seen that true holiness in man is the perfect oneness of His will with that of God. Throughout our Lord's life, beginning with the temptation in the wilderness, He had subjected His will to the will of His Father and had consecrated Himself as a sacrifice to God. But it was chiefly in Gethsemane that He did this. That was the hour and the power of darkness; the temptation to put away the terrible cup of wrath from His lips and to do His own will came with almost irresistible power, but He rejected the temptation. He offered Himself and His will to the will and holiness of God. He sanctified Himself by a perfect oneness of will with that of God.

This sanctification of Himself has become the power by which we may be sanctified through the truth. This is in perfect agreement with the epistle to the Hebrews where, speaking of the words used by Christ, we read: *I come to do thy will, O God,* and then it is added, *In this will, we are sanctified through the offering of the body of Jesus, the Christ, once for all* (Hebrews 10:9-10). It was because the offering of His body was His surrender of Himself to do the will of God that we become sanctified by that will. He sanctified Himself for us that we might be sanctified through the truth. The perfect obedience of Jesus was not only the meritorious cause of our salvation but also *the power* by which sin was forever conquered. *But this man, after he had offered one sacrifice for sins for ever, . . . For by one offering he has perfected for ever those that are sanctified* (Hebrews 10:12, 14).

The true relationship of our Lord to His own people is even more evident after hearing of how becoming it was that our Lord should suffer as He did. We read: *For both he that sanctifies and those who are sanctified are all of one* (Hebrews 2:11). The unity between the Lord Jesus and His people consists in the fact that they both receive their life from one Father, and both have a share in the same sanctification. Jesus is the sanctifier; they become the sanctified. Sanctification is the bond that unites them. *Therefore, Jesus also, that he might sanctify the people with his own blood, suffered outside the gate* (Hebrews 13:12).

If we are willing to understand and experience what sanctification by the blood means, then it is of the utmost importance for us first to grasp the fact that sanctification is the characteristic and purpose of the entire sufferings of our Lord, which provided the fruit and means of blessing. His sanctification has the characteristic of those sufferings and therein lay its value and power. Our sanctification is the purpose of those sufferings; only in attaining that purpose do they work out the perfect blessing.

It was as the Holy One that God foreordained redemption. His will was to glorify His holiness in victory over sin by the sanctification of man after His own image. With the same objective that our Lord Jesus endured and accomplished His sufferings, we must be consecrated to God. And if the Holy Spirit, the Holy God as Spirit, comes into us to reveal the redemption that is in Jesus, this continues to be the main objective with Him. As the Holy Spirit, He is the spirit of holiness.

Reconciliation, pardon, and cleansing from sin all have an unspeakable value; they all, however, point toward sanctification. God's will is that each one who has been marked by the precious blood should know that it is a divine mark, which characterizes his entire separation to God. This blood calls him to an undivided consecration to a life wholly for God, and this blood is the promise and the power of a participation in God's holiness through which God Himself will make His abiding place in him and be his God.

Oh, that we might understand and believe: *Jesus also, that he might sanctify the people with his own blood, suffered outside the gate* (Hebrews 13:12).

How Sanctification is Obtained

In general, an answer to this question is that everyone who partakes of the blood also partakes of sanctification and is a sanctified person in God's eyes.

Man continues to experience the blood's sanctifying effects in proportion to how close he walks with God, even though he still understands little of how those effects are produced. Let no one think that he must first understand how to acquire or explain everything before he may pray that the blood reveal its sanctifying power in him. No, it was in connection with the rite of cleansing, the washing of the disciples' feet, that the Lord Jesus said, *What I do thou dost not understand now, but thou shalt understand afterwards* (John 13:7). The Lord Jesus Himself sanctifies His people by His own blood. The man who gives himself to worship and communicate with the Lamb will experience through the Lamb's blood a sanctification beyond his comprehension. The Lord Jesus will do this for him.

But the believer needs to grow in knowledge also, because only in this way can he enter into the full blessing which is prepared for him. We have both the right and the duty to inquire about the essential connection between the benefit of the blood and our sanctification. We can know in what way the Lord Jesus will work those things in us, which we have learned to be the chief qualities of sanctification.

We have seen that the beginning of all sanctification is separation to God as His possession to be at His disposal. Isn't this just what the blood proclaims? That the power of sin is broken; we are loosed from its bonds; we are no longer its bondservants; but we belong to Him who purchased our freedom with His blood. *Ye are bought with a price, therefore glorify God in your body and in your spirit, which are God's* (1 Corinthians 6:20). This is the language which tells us that we are God's possession. Because He desires to have us entirely for Himself, He has chosen us, bought us, and set upon us the distinguishing mark of the blood to live only for His service. The idea of separation is clearly expressed in the words we often repeat, *Jesus also, that he might sanctify the people with his own blood, suffered outside the gate. Let us go forth, therefore, unto him outside the camp, bearing his reproach* (Hebrews 13:12-13). *Going out* from all that is of this world was the characteristic of Him who was holy and undefiled, separate from sinners, and this must be the characteristic of all His followers.

As a believer, the Lord Jesus has sanctified you through His own blood, and He desires you to experience the full power of that sanctification. Endeavour to gain a clear impression of what has taken place in you through that blood. The Holy God desires to have you entirely for Himself. No one, nothing, may have the least right over you, nor *do you* have any right over yourself. God has separated you unto Himself, and He has set His mark upon you – the blood of Jesus. That blood is the life of the eternal Son of God, the blood that on the throne of grace is always before God's face. This blood assures us of full redemption from the power of sin and is a sign that we belong to God.

Let every thought about the blood awaken in you the glorious confession, "By His own blood, the Lord Jesus has sanctified me; He has taken complete possession of me for God, and I belong entirely to God."

We have seen that sanctification is more than separation, which is only the beginning. We have also seen that personal consecration and hearty, willing surrender to live only for and in God's holy will is part of sanctification.

In what way can the blood of Christ work this surrender in us and sanctify us in that surrender? The answer is not difficult. It is not enough to believe in the power of the blood to redeem us and to free us from sin, but we must, above all, notice the source of this power.

We know that it has this power because of the willingness of the Lord Jesus when He surrendered Himself. In shedding His blood, He sanctified Himself and offered Himself entirely to God and His holiness. This is what makes the blood so holy; it possesses the sanctifying power. In the blood we have a representation of the utter self-surrender of Christ. The blood speaks of the consecration of Jesus to the Father as the opening of the way and supplying the power for victory over sin. The closer we come in contact with the blood and the more we live under the realization of having been sprinkled by the blood, the more we shall hear the voice of the blood, declaring that "Entire surrender to God is the way to full redemption from sin."

The voice of the blood will not speak simply to teach us or to awaken thought; the blood speaks with a divine and life-giving power. It works out in us the same perspective that was in our Lord Jesus. By His own blood, Jesus sanctifies us that we might hold nothing back and surrender ourselves with all our hearts to the holy will of God.

But consecration itself, even along with and following separation, is still only a preparation. Complete sanctification takes place when God takes possession of the temple and fills it with His glory. *There will I testify of myself unto the sons of Israel, and the place shall be sanctified with my glory* (Exodus 29:43). Actual, complete sanctification consists of God imparting His own holiness – Himself.

The blood speaks here. It tells us that heaven is opened; the powers of the heavenly life have come down to earth; every hindrance has been removed, and God can make His abode with man.

Immediate nearness and fellowship with God are made possible by the blood. The believer who surrenders himself unreservedly to the blood obtains the full assurance that God will give Himself and reveal His holiness in him.

How glorious are the results of such a sanctification. Through the Holy Spirit, the soul's communication is with the living God, accompanied by the tenderest caution against sin and guarded by the fear of God.

But to live in watchfulness against sin does not satisfy the soul. The temple must not only be cleansed, but it must also be filled with God's glory. All the virtues of divine holiness, as revealed in the Lord Jesus, are to be sought and found in fellowship with God. Sanctification means union with God – fellowship in His will, sharing His life, and conformity to His image.

Therefore, Jesus also, that he might sanctify the people with his own blood, suffered outside the gate. Let us go forth, therefore, unto him outside the camp (Hebrews 13:12-13). Yes, He is the One who sanctifies His people. *Let us go forth unto him.* Let us trust Him to make known to us the power of the blood.

Let us yield ourselves to its blessed effectiveness. That blood, through which He sanctified Himself, has entered heaven to open it for us. It can make our hearts a throne of God that the grace and glory of God may dwell in us. Yes, let us go forth unto him outside the camp. He who is willing to lose and say farewell to everything in order that Jesus may sanctify him will not fail to obtain the blessing. He who is willing at any cost to experience the full power of the precious blood can be assured that he will be sanctified by Jesus Himself through that blood.

May the God of peace sanctify you completely. Amen.

Chapter 6

Cleansed to Serve the Living God

*Now in Christ Jesus ye who at another time were
far off are made near by the blood of the Christ.*
(Ephesians 2:13)

*How much more shall the blood of Christ, . . .
purge your conscience . . . to serve the living God?*
(Hebrews 9:14)

Afer our study of sanctification through the blood, we
need to consider what the intimate communication with
God involves. Sanctification and intimacy are closely related
in Scripture. Without sanctification there can be no intimate
communication. How could one who is unholy have fellowship
with a holy God? On the other hand, without this communication there can be no growth in holiness; it is only in fellowship
with the Holy One that holiness can be found.

The intimate connection between sanctification and communication appears plainly in the story of the revolt of Nadab
and Abihu. God made this the occasion of a clear statement
about the peculiar nature of the priesthood in Israel. He said,
I will be sanctified in those that come near me (Leviticus 10:3).

Then again in the conspiracy of Korah against Moses and Aaron, Moses spoke for God and said, *Tomorrow the LORD will show who are his and who is holy and will cause the one who is holy to come near unto him; the one whom he has chosen he will cause to come near unto him* (Numbers 16:5).

We have already seen that God's election and separation unto Himself of His own are closely connected to sanctification. It is evident here also that the glory and blessing secured by this election to holiness is nothing more than communication and intimacy with God. To enjoy His love in this way is indeed the highest, the one perfect blessing for man, who was created for God. The psalmist sings: *Blessed is the man whom thou dost choose and cause to approach unto thee that he may dwell in thy courts* (Psalm 65:4). We see that consecration to God and nearness to Him are the same thing. The sprinkling of the blood that sanctifies man and takes possession of him for God grants him the right of communication.

The priests in Israel had this right. In the record of their consecration, we read: *And he [Moses] brought Aaron's sons, and Moses put of the blood upon the tip of their right ears and upon the thumbs of their right hands* (Leviticus 8:24). Those who belong to God may, and indeed must, live in nearness to Him; they belong to Him. This is illustrated in the case of our Lord, our Great High Priest, who *by his own blood he entered in once into the sanctuary* (Hebrews 9:12). It is the same with every believer, according to the Word: *Having therefore, brethren, boldness to enter into the sanctuary by the blood of Jesus, let us draw near . . . having our hearts purified from an evil conscience* (Hebrews 10:19, 22).

The word *enter*, as used in this verse, is the peculiar word used of the approach of the priest to God. In the same way, in the book of Revelation, our right to draw near as priests is declared to be by the power of the blood. We were redeemed from our sins by his own blood, who *hast made us unto our God kings and priests*, to him be the glory forever (Revelation 5:10). *These are those who came out of great tribulation and have washed their long robes, and made them white in the blood of the Lamb. Therefore, they are before the throne of God and serve him day and night in his temple* (Revelation 7:14-15).

One of the most glorious blessings made possible for us by the power of the blood is that of drawing near the throne into the very presence of God. To understand what this blessing means, let us consider what is contained in it.

It includes:

1. The right to dwell in the presence of God.

2. The privilege of offering spiritual sacrifices to God.

3. The power to acquire blessing for others.

The Right to Dwell in the Presence of God

Although this privilege belonged exclusively to the priests in Israel, we know that they had free access to the dwelling place of God. They had to abide there continually. As members of the household of God, they ate the showbread and partook of the sacrifices. A true Israelite thought there was no higher privilege than this. The psalmist expressed is as such: *Blessed* [happy] *is the man whom thou dost choose and cause to approach unto thee that he may dwell in thy courts: we shall be satisfied with the goodness of thy house even of thy holy temple* (Psalm 65:4).

It was because of the proven presence of God that believers in those days longed after the house of God with such strong desire. The cry was, *when shall I come and appear before God?* (Psalm 42:2). They understood something of the spiritual meaning of the privilege of drawing near to God. The psalmist says, *But as for me, to draw near to God is good; I have put my hope in the Lord GOD, that I may declare all thy works* (Psalm 73:28). It represented to them the enjoyment of His love, fellowship, protection, and blessing. They could exclaim, *Oh how great is thy goodness, which thou hast laid up for those that fear thee; . . . Thou shalt keep them in the secret place of thy face* (Psalm 31:19-20).

The precious blood of Christ has opened the way for the believer into God's presence, and communication with Him is a deep, spiritual reality. He who knows the full power of the blood is brought so near that he can always live in the immediate presence of God and in the enjoyment of the unspeakable blessings attached to it. The child of God has the assurance of God's love, and he experiences and enjoys it. God Himself imparts it. He lives daily in the friendship and fellowship of God. As God's child, he makes his thoughts and wishes known to the Father with perfect freedom. In this communication with God, he possesses all that he needs; he lacks no good thing. His soul is kept in perfect rest and peace, because God is with him. He receives all required direction and teaching. God's eye is always on him and guiding him. Through communication with God, he is able to hear the softest whispers of the Holy Spirit. He learns to understand the slightest sign of his Father's will, and he follows it. His strength continually increases, for God is his strength, and God is always with him.

Fellowship with God exerts a wonderful influence on the believer's life and character. The presence of God fills him with humility, fear, and holy caution. He lives as in the presence of a king. Fellowship with God produces godlike attitudes in him. Beholding the image of God, he is changed into the same image. Dwelling with the Holy One makes him holy. He can say, *To draw near to God is good; I have put my hope in the Lord GOD* (Psalm 73:28). O you who are the children of the new covenant, don't you have a thousand times more reasons to speak of this now that the veil has been rent asunder and the way opened for living in God's holy presence? May this high privilege awaken our desires. Communication with God, fellowship with God, dwelling with God and He with us. May we never be satisfied with anything less. This is the true Christian life.

But intimacy with God is not only blessed because of the salvation enjoyed in it, but also from the service that may be rendered because of that closeness.

Let us therefore consider:

The Privilege of Offering Spiritual Sacrifices to God

Our service of bringing spiritual sacrifices to God is a further privilege. The enjoyment of the priests in drawing near to God in His dwelling place was secondary to something higher. They were servants of the Holy Place to bring what belonged to God into His house. Only as they found joy in drawing near to God could that service become truly blessed.

The service consisted of bringing in the blood of sprinkling, the preparation of the incense to fill the house with its fragrance, and the ordering of everything that pertained to the arrangement of His house according to God's word.

They had to guard, serve, and provide for the dwelling place of the Most High, so it would be worthy of Him and of His glory, so His good pleasure might be fulfilled. If the blood of Jesus brings us near, we should live before God as His servants and bring Him the spiritual sacrifices which are pleasing in His sight.

The priests brought the blood into the Holy Place before God. In our communication with God, we can bring no offering more pleasing to Him than a believing heart that honors the blood of the Lamb. Every act of humble trust or hearty thanksgiving of the blood is acceptable to Him. Our abiding and communication from hour to hour must be a glorifying of the blood before God. The priests brought the incense into the Holy Place to fill God's house with fragrance. The prayers of God's people are the delightful incense with which He desires to be surrounded in His habitation. The value of prayer does not consist merely in its being the means of obtaining things we need. No, it has a higher aim than that. Prayer is a ministry of God in which He delights.

The life of a believer who enjoys drawing near to God through the blood is a life of unceasing prayer. In a deep sense of dependence, grace is sought and expected for each moment and each step. In the blessed conviction of God's nearness and unchanging goodness, the soul pours itself out in confidence that every promise will be fulfilled. In the midst of the joy that the light of God's face brings, there arises thanksgiving and adoration along with prayer.

These are the spiritual offerings – the perpetual offerings of the priests of God. They have been sanctified and brought near by the blood, so they might always live and walk in His presence.

But there is more. The priests had the duty to attend to everything for cleansing or provision that was necessary in the ministry of the temple. What is the ministry now under the new covenant? Thanks be to God, there are no outward or exclusive arrangements for divine worship. No, the Father has determined that whatever anyone does who is walking in His presence is a spiritual offering. If a believer walks as in God's presence, whatever he offers is a service to God; it is a priestly sacrifice, well pleasing to God. *Whether therefore ye eat or drink or whatever ye do, do everything to the glory of God* (1 Corinthians 10:31). *And whatever ye do whether in word or deed, do all in the name of the Lord Jesus, giving thanks to the God and Father by him* (Colossians 3:17). In this way, all our actions become thank offerings to God.

How little Christians recognize the glory of a life of complete devotion, always in communication with God. Because I'm cleansed, sanctified, and brought near by the power of the blood, my earthly calling, my whole life, even my eating and drinking are a spiritual service. My work, my business, my money, and my house become sanctified by the presence of God, because I walk in His presence. The poorest earthly work is a priestly service, because it is performed by a priest in God's temple.

But even this does not exhaust the glory of the blessing of communication with God. The highest blessing of the priesthood is that the priest appears as the representative of others before God.

The Power to Acquire Blessing for Others

This is what gives glory to the nearness of God. In Israel, the priests were the mediators between God and the people. They carried the sins and needs of the people into the presence of God; they obtained the power to declare the pardon for sin and the right to bless the people from God.

This privilege now belongs to all believers as the priestly family of the new covenant. When God permitted His redeemed ones to approach Him through the blood, it was so He might bless them that they might become a blessing to others. Priestly mediation, a priestly heart that can have sympathy with those who are weak, is a priestly power to obtain the blessing of God in the temple and convey it to others. In these things, communication, the drawing near to God through the blood, demonstrates its highest power and glory.

We can exercise our priestly dignity in a twofold manner:

By Intercession

The ministry of intercession is one of the highest privileges of the child of God. It does not mean that we pour out our wishes in prayer to God and ask for the necessary supply. That is good as far as it goes and brings a blessing with it. But the peculiar ministry of intercession is something more wonderful and finds its power in the *prayer of faith*. This *prayer of faith* is different from the outpouring of our wishes to God and leaving them with Him.

In the true *prayer of faith*, the intercessor must spend time with God to appropriate the promises of His Word and permit himself to be taught by the Holy Spirit to know whether the promises can be applied to this particular case. He takes upon himself, as a burden, the sin and need, which are the subject of prayer, and claims the promise concerning it. He remains in the presence of God until God awakens the faith that the prayer has been heard.

In this way, parents sometimes pray for their children; ministers for their congregations; laborers in God's vineyard for the souls committed to them, until they know that their prayers are heard. The blood is what has the power to bring us near to God and grant the liberty to pray until the answer is obtained.

Oh, if we understood more perfectly what it means to dwell in the presence of God, we would demonstrate more power in the exercise of our holy priesthood.

Instrumentality

A further expression of our role is that we not only intercede for others, but we also become the instruments by whom a blessing is ministered. Every believer is called, and he feels himself compelled by love to labor on behalf of others. *God was in Christ, reconciling the world unto himself, not imputing their trespasses unto them and having placed in us the word of reconciliation. Now then we are ambassadors for Christ, as though God did exhort you by us* (2 Corinthians 5:19-20).

Believers know that God has blessed them that they might be a blessing to others, but they seem to have no power for this work of bringing blessing to others. They say they are not able to exercise an influence over others with their words. This is not surprising if they do not dwell in the sanctuary. We read that *the LORD separated the tribe of Levi . . . to stand before the LORD . . . and to bless in his name* (Deuteronomy 10:8). The priestly *power* of blessing depends on the priest-like *life* in the presence of God. He who experiences the power of the blood to preserve him will have courage to believe that the blood can deliver others. The holy, life-giving power of the blood will create in him the same result as through Jesus's sacrifice of Himself to redeem others.

As we communicate with God, His love will set our love on fire, and He will strengthen our belief that He will surely make use of us. The spirit of Jesus will take possession of us to enable us to labor in humility, wisdom, and power; our weakness and poverty become the vessels in which God's power can work. From our words and example, blessings will flow, because we dwell with Him who is pure blessing, and He will not permit anyone to be near Him without also being filled with His blessing.

Beloved, isn't the life prepared for us a glorious and blessed one? The enjoyment of the nearness to God, the performance of the ministry of His house, and the imparting of His blessing to others are blessings.

Let no one think that the full blessing is not for him or that such a life is too high for him. In the power of Jesus's blood, we have the assurance that drawing near is for us also, so *draw near to God, and he will draw near to you* (James 4:8).

For those who truly desire this blessing, I give the following advice:

First, remember that this power is designed for all of us. All who are God's children have been brought near by the blood. All can desire the full experience of it. Remember that the life in communication and nearness with God is for all of us. The Father doesn't want any of His children to be far off. We cannot please our God as we ought, if we live without this blessing. Grace to live as priests is prepared for us; free entrance into the sanctuary as our abiding place is for us. We can be assured of this, for God bestows on us His holy presence, His indwelling as our right as His children. Let us embrace this truth.

Then, we must seek to make the full power of the blood our own possession. That power makes communication and intimacy possible. Our hearts can be filled with faith in the power of the blood of reconciliation. Sin has been so entirely atoned for and blotted out that its power to keep us away from God has been completely removed. Live in the joyful profession that sin is powerless to separate us for even one moment from God. By the blood we have been fully justified and thus have a righteous claim to a place in the sanctuary. The blood will cleanse us, so we can expect the fellowship that follows and the inner deliverance from the defilement of sin. May we repeat with the writer of the book of Hebrews: *how much more shall the blood of the Christ, who through the eternal Spirit offered himself without spot to God, purge your conscience from the works of death to serve the living God?* (Hebrews 9:14). We must let the blood sanctify us and separate us for God to be filled by Him. Let the pardoning, cleansing, and sanctifying power of the blood guide and direct us. This will automatically bring us near to God and protect us.

And last, we must not hesitate to expect that Jesus will reveal the power of the blood to bring us near to God.

The blood was shed to unite us to God.

The blood has accomplished its work, and it will perfect it in us.

The blood has unspeakable virtue and glory in God's sight.

God draws near with joy and good pleasure to the heart

that surrenders itself entirely to the complete effectiveness of the blood. The blood has irresistible power. Be assured that the blood is able to preserve us every day in God's presence by its divine life-giving power. Our abiding with God is as sure and certain as the blood is precious and all powerful.

They *have washed their long robes, and made them white in the blood of the Lamb. Therefore, they are before the throne of God and serve him day and night in his temple* (Revelation 7:14-15). That eternal glory also affects our lives on earth. The fuller our faith and experience of the power of the blood, the closer our intimacy and assurance of nearness to the throne. Unbroken ministry of God widens and the power to serve the living God increases. O Lord, may this word have its full power over us now, here and hereafter!

Chapter 7

Dwelling in the Holiest

Having therefore, brethren, boldness to enter into the sanctuary by the blood of Jesus, by a new and living way, which he has consecrated for us, through the veil, that is to say, his flesh; and having that great priest over the house of God, let us draw near with a true heart in full assurance of faith, having our hearts purified from an evil conscience and our bodies washed with pure water. (Hebrews 10:19-22)

I n these words, we have a summary of the main points of this epistle and of the good news about God's grace, as the Holy Spirit caused it to be presented to the Hebrews and then to us.

Through sin, man was driven out of paradise and away from the presence and fellowship of God. In His mercy God sought to restore the broken fellowship from the beginning. Through the symbolic types in the tabernacle, He gave Israel the expectation of a time to come when the wall of partition would be removed and His people might dwell in His presence. *When shall I come and appear before God?* was the longing sigh of the saints of the old covenant (Psalm 42:2).

Many of God's children under the new covenant also sigh because they do not understand that the way into the holiest place has been opened and every child of God may have his real dwelling place there.

For those who long to experience the full power of redemption, let's take note of what our God says to us about the Holy Place and our freedom to enter through the blood. Hebrews 10:19-22 shows us what God has prepared for us; then we learn how we prepare to enter into that fellowship and to live in it.

Read the text again with attention and see that the words *let us draw near* are the center of it all. The following outline may be helpful:

1. What God has prepared for us.

   The sanctuary.
   Liberty through the Blood.
   A new and living way.
   A Great Priest.

2. How we are prepared.

   With a true heart.
   In full assurance of faith.
   The cleansed heart.
   The washed body.

Read the text again with an eye on this outline:

> *Having therefore, brethren, boldness to enter into the **sanctuary** by the **blood of Jesus**, by a **new and living way**, which he has **consecrated** for us, through the veil, that is to say, his flesh; and having that **great priest** over the house of God, let us draw near with a **true heart** in **full assurance of***

*faith, having our **hearts purified from an evil conscience** and our **bodies washed with pure** water.* (Hebrews 10:19-22 emphasis added)

What God Has Prepared for Us

The Sanctuary

> *Having therefore, brethren, boldness to enter into the sanctuary by the blood of Jesus, . . . let us draw near.*

To bring us into the sanctuary is the end of the redemptive work of Jesus, and whoever does not know what the sanctuary is cannot enjoy the full benefit of redemption.

What is this sanctuary or Holy Place? It is where God dwells; the sanctuary is the dwelling place of the Most High. This doesn't only refer to heaven, but also to the *spiritual* holiest place of God's presence.

Under the old covenant, there was a physical sanctuary, the dwelling place of God in which the priests entered into God's presence and served Him:

> *Nevertheless the first* [covenant] *had its justifications of worship and its worldly sanctuary. For there was a tabernacle made: the first, in which was the lampstand and the table and the showbread, which is called the sanctuary. And after the second veil was the tabernacle which is called the Holy of Holies, . . . the priests went always into the first tabernacle, accomplishing the service of God. But into the second the high priest went alone once every year, not without blood, which he offered for his own ignorance, and for that of the people: The Holy Spirit signifying in this, that the way into the sanctuary*

THE POWER OF THE BLOOD

*was not yet made manifest, as long as the first tab-
ernacle was yet standing.* (Hebrews 9:1-3, 6-8)

Under the new covenant is the true *spiritual* tabernacle, which is not confined to any place. The Holiest is where God reveals Himself. *True worshippers shall worship the Father in spirit and in truth, for the Father seeks such to worship him. God is a Spirit and those that worship him must worship him in spirit and in truth* (John 4:23-24). We also know that *ye are the temple of the living God; as God has said, I will dwell in them and walk in them and I will be their God, and they shall be my people* (2 Corinthians 6:16).

What a glorious privilege it is to enter into the Holiest and dwell there – to walk all day in the presence of God. What a rich blessing is poured out there. In this sanctuary, we can enjoy the favor and fellowship of God; we experience the life and bless-ing of God, and we find His power and the joy of God. We can spend our lives in the purity and consecration of the Holiest; the incense of sweet savor is burned and sacrifices acceptable to God are offered. It is a holy life of prayer and blessedness.

Under the old covenant, everything was physical; the sanc-tuary was made of local, physical materials. Under the new covenant, everything is spiritual, and the true sanctuary owes its existence to the power of the Holy Spirit. Through the Holy Spirit, a real life in the Holiest is possible, and the knowledge that God dwells there can be as certain as the priests of old entering the Holy Place. The Spirit makes the work that Jesus has accomplished indisputable in our experience.

As one who has been redeemed, it is a fitting thing for you to make your home in the Holiest, for Christ cannot reveal the full power of His redemption elsewhere. But in the Holiest He can bless you richly. Oh, understand this, and let the objective of God and of our Lord Jesus be yours also. May it be the one desire of our hearts to enter into, to live in, and to minister in the Holiest. We can confidently expect the Holy Spirit to give us a correct understanding of the glory of entering into a dwelling – the sanctuary.

Liberty through the Blood

Admission to the Holiest belongs to God. He thought of it and prepared it; we have the liberty, the freedom, and the right to enter by the blood of Jesus, which exercises such a wonderful power that a son of perdition may receive full freedom to enter into the divine sanctuary through it. *Ye who at another time were far off are made near by the blood of the Christ* (Ephesians 2:13).

And what gives the blood this wonderful power? Scripture says *the soul (or life) of the flesh is in the blood* (Leviticus 17:11). The power of the blood is in the value of the life. The power of the divine life dwelt and worked in the blood of Jesus.

But that power could not be exercised for reconciliation until it was first shed. By bearing the punishment of sin by His death, the Lord Jesus conquered the power of sin and brought it to nothing. *The power of sin is the law*, and by perfectly fulfilling the law when He shed His blood under its curse, He made sin entirely powerless. So the blood has its wonderful power, not only because the life of God's Son was in it, but also because it was given as an atonement for sin. This is the reason Scripture speaks so highly about the blood. Through the blood of the everlasting covenant, God has *brought again from the dead our Lord Jesus* (Hebrews 13:20).

By his own blood he entered in once into the sanctuary designed for eternal redemption (Hebrews 9:12). The power of the blood has destroyed the power of sin, death, the grave, and hell, and the power of the blood has opened heaven's doors.

And now we have liberty to enter through the blood. Sin took away our liberty to approach God; the blood perfectly restores this liberty to us. Whoever takes time to meditate upon the power of that blood and believes it for himself will obtain a wonderful view of the liberty and directness with which we can now have communication and intimacy with God.

Oh, the divine, wonderful power of the blood! Through the blood we enter into the Holiest. The blood pleads for us with an eternal, ceaseless effect. It removes sin from God's sight and from our conscience. Every moment we have free, full entrance, and we can approach God and commune with Him through the blood.

Oh, that the Holy Spirit might reveal to us the full power of the blood! Under His teaching what a complete access we enjoy for intimate fellowship with the Father! Our life is in the Holiest through the blood.

A New and Living Way
Having therefore, brethren, boldness to enter into the sanctuary by the blood of Jesus by a new and living way, which he has consecrated for us, through the veil, that is to say, his flesh, the blood bestows our right of entrance (Hebrews 10:19-20). The way, as a living and life-giving one, bestows the power. He has consecrated this way by His flesh, but this does not mean it is merely a repetition in other words of the same thought as *through His blood*. By no means.

Jesus shed His blood for us; in this we cannot follow Him. But the way by which He walked when He shed His blood, the rending of the veil of His flesh, in that way we *must* follow Him. What He did in the opening of that way is a living power that draws and carries us as we enter the sanctuary. The lesson we have to learn here is that the way into the sanctuary is through the rent veil of the flesh.

The veil that separated God and us was the flesh. Sin has its power in the flesh; only through the taking away of sin could the veil be removed. When Jesus came in the flesh, He could rend the veil only by dying and so conquer the power of the flesh and sin. He offered up the flesh and delivered it to death. This is what gave worth and power to the shedding of His blood.

And this remains now the law for each one who desires to enter the sanctuary through His blood; it must be through the rent veil of the flesh. The blood demands and the blood accomplishes the rending of the flesh. Where the blood of Jesus works powerfully, there follows the putting to death of the flesh. He who desires to spare the flesh cannot enter into the Holiest. The flesh must be sacrificed – given over to death.

In proportion as the believer perceives the sinfulness of his flesh and puts to death all that is in the flesh, he will better understand the power of the blood. The believer doesn't do this in his own strength; he comes by a living way which Jesus has consecrated; the life-giving power of Jesus works in this way. The Christian is crucified and dead with Jesus; they that are Christ's have crucified the flesh. The apostle Paul tells us, *I am crucified with Christ; nevertheless I live; yet not I, but Christ lives in me, and the life which I now live in the flesh I live by the faith of the Son of God, who loved me and gave himself for me* (Galatians 2:20). It is in fellowship with Christ that we enter through the veil.

Oh, glorious way, *the new and living way,* full of life-giving power, which Christ has consecrated for us! By this way we have the liberty to enter into the sanctuary through the blood of Jesus. May the Lord God lead us along this way through the rent veil, through the death of the flesh, to the full life of the Spirit; then we shall find our dwelling place within the veil in the sanctuary with God. Each sacrifice of the flesh leads us through the blood and further into the sanctuary.

Compare this further with 1 Peter 3:18 which says, *Christ . . . being put to death in the flesh,* and 1 Peter 4:1 which says,

Christ has suffered for us in the flesh that we might live in the Spirit. God sent *his own Son in the likeness of sinful flesh and for sin, condemned sin in the flesh that the righteousness of the law might be fulfilled in us who walk not according to the flesh, but according to the Spirit* (Romans 8:3-4).

The Great Priest

And having that great high priest over the house of God, let us draw near with a true heart in full assurance of faith. (Hebrews 10:21-22)

Praise God, we have not only the work but also the living person of Christ as we enter the sanctuary; not only the blood and the living way, but Jesus Himself as High Priest over the house of God.

The priests who went into the earthly sanctuary could do so only because of their relationship to the High Priest; none but the sons of Aaron were priests. We have an entrance into the sanctuary because of our relationship to the Lord Jesus. He said to the Father, Behold here am I, and the children *whom thou hast given me* (John 17:11).

He is the Great High Priest. The epistle to the Hebrews has shown us that He is the true Melchizedek, the Eternal Son, who has an eternal and changeless priesthood, and as High Priest He is seated on the throne. He lives there to pray always; *therefore He is able also to save to the uttermost those that come unto God by him* (Hebrews 7:25). A great and all-powerful High Priest He is.

As the High Priest over the house of God, He is appointed over the entire ministry of the house of God. All the people of God are under His care. If we desire to enter the sanctuary, He is there to receive us and to present us to the Father. He Himself will complete in us the sprinkling of the blood. Through the blood He has entered; through the blood He also brings us in. He will teach us the duties and our communication there. He makes our prayers, our offerings, and the duties of our ministry acceptable, however weak they are. What is more, He presents us with heavenly light and heavenly power for our work and life in the sanctuary. Just as His blood obtained access, His sacrifice of His flesh is the living way. As we enter, He keeps us abiding there and able to walk well-pleasing to God. As the sympathetic High Priest, He knows how to stoop to each one, even the weakest. That is what makes communion with God in the sanctuary so attractive; we find Jesus there as the High Priest over the house of God.

And when it seems as if the Holiest is too high or too holy for us and we cannot understand what the power of the blood is or how we are to walk on the new and living way, we may look up to the living Savior Himself to teach us and to bring us into the sanctuary. He is the High Priest over the house of God.

Let us draw near to where God waits for us; the blood gives us liberty, the living way carries us, and the High Priest helps us. Let nothing hold us back from making use of these wonderful blessings which God has designed for us. Our right has been obtained for us by the blood of Jesus; by His own footsteps He has consecrated the way. He lives in His eternal priesthood to receive us and to sanctify, preserve, and bless us. Let us no longer hesitate or turn back. Let us sacrifice all for this one thing in view of what God has prepared for us. *Let us draw near* by the hand of Jesus to appear before our Father and to find our life in the light of His countenance.

But can we know how to be prepared to enter? Our text gives us a glorious answer to this question.

How We Are Prepared

With a True Heart

This is the first of the four demands made on the believer who wishes *to draw near*. It is coupled with the second demand, *full assurance of faith*, and it is chiefly in its connection with the second that we understand what *a true heart* means.

The preaching of the gospel begins with repentance and faith. Man cannot receive God's grace by faith, if at the same time sin is not forsaken. In the progress of the life of faith, this law is always binding. The full assurance of faith cannot be reached without *a true heart* – a heart that is wholly honest with God and surrendered entirely to Him. The Holiest cannot be entered without *a true heart* – a heart that is truly desirous of seeking what it professes to seek.

Let us draw near with a true heart – a heart that truly desires to forsake everything to dwell in the Holiest – forsaking everything to possess God. A true heart abandons everything in order to yield itself to the authority and power of the blood. A true heart chooses *the new and living way* in order to go through the veil with Christ by the rending of the flesh. A true heart gives itself entirely to the indwelling and lordship of Jesus.

Let us draw near with a true heart. Without a true heart there is no entrance into the Holiest.

But who has a true heart? The new heart that God has given is a true heart. *Therefore if anyone is in Christ, they are a new creation: old things are passed away; behold, all things are made new* (2 Corinthians 5:17). By the power of the Spirit of God who dwells in that new heart, you can place yourself on the side of God against the sin that is still in your flesh. Tell the Lord Jesus, the High Priest, that you submit and cast down before Him every sin and all of your self-life, as you forsake all to follow Him.

And as regards the hidden depths of sin in your flesh, of

which you are not yet conscious, and the malice of your heart – for them also provision is made. King David wrote, *Search me, O God, and know my heart* (Psalm 139:23). Subject yourself continually to the heart-searching light of the Spirit. He will uncover what is hidden from you. He who does this has a true heart to enter into the Holiest.

Let's not be afraid to tell God that we draw near with a true heart. Let's be assured that God will not judge us according to the perfection of what we do, but according to the honesty with which we forsake every known sin and accept conviction by the Holy Spirit of all our hidden sin. A heart that does this honestly is a true heart in God's sight. We can approach the Holiest with a true heart through the blood. Praise God, through His Spirit we have a true heart.

In Full Assurance of Faith

We know what place faith occupies in God's dealings with man. *Without faith it is impossible to please God* (Hebrews 11:6). Here at the entrance into the Holiest, everything depends on the full assurance of faith.

We must have a full assurance of faith that a Holy Place exists where we can dwell and walk with God and where the power of the precious blood has conquered sin so perfectly that nothing can prevent our undisturbed fellowship with God. The way that Jesus sanctified through His flesh is *a living way,* which carries those who tread on it with eternal living power. This is where the Great High Priest over the house of God can save to the uttermost those who come to God through Him; by His Spirit He works in us everything that is needful for life in the Holiest. We must believe these things and hold fast in the full assurance of faith.

But how can we get to this point? How can our faith grow to this full assurance? By fellowship with *Jesus, the author and finisher of our faith* (Hebrews 12:2). As the Great High Priest over the house of God, He enables us to appropriate faith. By considering Him, His wonderful love, His perfect work, and His precious and all-powerful blood, faith is sustained and strengthened. God has given Him to us to awaken our faith. By keeping our eyes fixed on Him, faith and the full assurance of faith become ours.

In handling the Word of God, remember that *faith comes by hearing, and the ear to hear by the word of God* (Romans 10:17). Faith comes by the Word and grows by the Word, but not the Word as law but as the voice of Jesus. *The words that I have spoken unto you, they are Spirit and they are life* (John 6:63). Take time to meditate on the Word and treasure it in your heart but always with a heart set on Jesus Himself. It is faith in Jesus that saves. The Word that is taken to Jesus in prayer and talked over with Him is the Word that is effective.

Remember that *for whosoever has, to him shall be given* (Matthew 13:12). Make use of the faith that you have; exercise it, declare it, and let your believing trust in God become the mission of your life. God wants children who believe Him; He desires nothing so much as faith. Make it your habit to exercise trust in God's guidance and God's blessing in everything.

To enter into the Holiest, full assurance of faith is necessary. *Let us draw near in full assurance of faith.* Redemption through the blood is perfect and powerful; the love and grace of Jesus is overflowing; the blessedness of dwelling in the Holiest is surely for us and within our reach. Let us draw near in full assurance of faith.

The Cleansed Heart

The heart is the center of human life, and the conscience is the center of the heart. Through his conscience, man recognizes his relationship to God; it tells him when all is not right between

God and himself – not merely that he commits sin, but that he is sinful and alienated from God. A clear conscience bears witness that he is pleasing to God (Hebrews 11:5). It bears witness not only that his sins are forgiven but also that his heart is sincere before God. He who desires to enter the Holiest must have his heart *cleansed from an evil conscience.* The words are translated *our hearts purified from an evil conscience.* The sprinkling of the blood accomplishes this cleansing and will purify your conscience to serve the living God.

We have already seen that access to the Holiest is by the blood. But that is not enough. There is a twofold sprinkling: the priests who drew near to God were not only reconciled through the sprinkling of blood before God on the altar, but also their very persons had to be sprinkled with the blood. The blood of Jesus must be brought by the Holy Spirit into direct contact with our hearts to cleanse them from an evil conscience. The blood removes all self-condemnation. It cleanses the conscience, which then witnesses the complete removal of guilt. There is no longer the least separation between God and us. The conscience bears witness that we are pleasing to God, our heart is cleansed, and we are in true living fellowship with God. Yes, the blood of Jesus Christ cleanses from all sin – not only from the guilt but also from the stain of sin.

Through the power of the blood, our fallen nature is prevented from exercising its power. Just as a fountain cleanses the grass with its gentle spray and keeps it fresh and green, so the blood works with a ceaseless effect to keep the soul clean. A heart that lives under the full power of the blood is a clean heart, cleansed from a guilty conscience and prepared to draw near with perfect freedom. The whole heart, the whole inner being, is cleansed by a divine operation.

Let us draw near, having our hearts purified from an evil conscience. Let us *in full assurance of faith* believe that our hearts are cleansed. Let us honor the blood by confessing before God that it cleanses us. The High Priest will make us understand the full meaning and power of the words *having the heart cleansed by the blood*. We gain access to the Holy Place prepared through the blood, and our hearts are prepared by the blood for that encounter. Oh, how glorious to have our hearts cleansed and to abide in the Holiest.

The Washed Body
We belong to two worlds, the seen and the unseen. We have an inner, hidden life that brings us in touch with God and an outer, bodily life by which we are in relationship with man. If this word refers to the body, it refers to the entire life in the body with all its activities.

The heart must be sprinkled with blood; the body must be washed with pure water. When the priests were consecrated, they were washed with water as well as sprinkled with blood:

> *And Aaron and his sons thou shalt bring unto the door of the tabernacle of the testimony and shalt wash them with water.* (Exodus 29:4)

> *And thou shalt take of the blood that shall be upon the altar and of the anointing oil and sprinkle it upon Aaron and upon his garments and upon his sons and upon their garments, and he shall be sanctified, and his garments and his sons and his sons' garments with him.* (Exodus 29:21)

And if they went into the Holy Place, there was not only the altar with its blood, but also the laver with its water.[3] So also

---

3   "As a Jewish person came into the outer courtyard, he saw the brazen altar. He had to bring an animal to the altar, which had a ramp in front of it. The brass of the altar was made of iron and copper, was very shiny, and gave a reflection. So as the man walked up the ramp and stood before the altar, he saw his own face. He recognized that he should be on the altar, not the innocent lamb. The copper in the altar speaks of being pliable, and the iron speaks of being strong.

Christ came by water and blood: *This is Jesus, the Christ, who came by water and blood; not by water only, but by water and blood* (1 John 5:6). *Christ also loved the congregation* [church] *and gave himself for her, that he might sanctify and cleanse her in the washing of water by the word, that he might present her glorious for himself, a congregation, not having spot or wrinkle or any such thing, but that she should be holy and without blemish* (Ephesians 5:25-27). Jesus had His baptism with water and later with blood (Luke 12:50).

There is for us also a twofold cleansing – with water and blood. Baptism with water is unto repentance for laying aside of sin; the apostle Paul declared, *Be baptized and wash away thy sins* (Acts 22:15-17). While the blood cleanses the heart and the inner man, baptism is the yielding of the body with all its visible life to separation from sin.

So, *let us draw near with a true heart in full assurance of faith, having our hearts purified from an evil conscience and our bodies washed with pure water* (Hebrews 10:22). The divine work of cleansing is through the sprinkling of blood; the human work of cleansing is through forsaking sin; these are inseparable.

We must be clean to enter into the Holiest. Just as we would never dream of approaching a king unwashed, so we would not come into the presence of God in the Holy Place without being cleansed from every sin. In the blood of Christ, God has given us the power to cleanse ourselves. Our desire to live with God in the Holiest must be united with forsaking even the least sin. The unclean may not enter the Holiest.

Praise God, He desires to have us there and to minister to Him. He desires our purity that we may enjoy His blessing – His

---

God's judgment is strong, but if we repent, it is pliable. After the sacrifice was made on the brazen altar, the person moved to the laver and washed his hands. He was washing the guilt from his hands" (Leviticus 16:15-22). From Rabbi Greg Hershberg, *A Life for God* (Abbotsford, WI: Aneko Press, 2017), 66-67.

Holy fellowship. He has provided through the blood and by the Spirit for us to be clean.

Let Us Draw Near

The Holiest Place is open even for those in our congregations who have not yet turned to the Lord. For them also the sanctuary has been opened. The precious blood, the living way, and the High Priest are for them also. With great confidence we dare to invite even them. My friends, if you are still far from God, don't despise God's wonderful grace any longer. Draw near to the Father who has so earnestly sent this invitation; at the cost of the blood of His Son, He has opened a way into the Holiest Place. He waits in love to receive you into His dwelling place as His child. Let us all draw near. Jesus Christ, the High Priest over the house of God, is a perfect Savior.

Let us draw near. The invitation comes specifically to all believers. Don't be satisfied to stand in the porch. It is not sufficient to hope that your sins are forgiven. Let us enter within the veil and in spirit press on to real nearness to our God. Let us live nearer to God, and wholly take our abode in His holy presence; our place is the innermost sanctuary.

Let us draw near with a true heart in full assurance of faith. He who gives himself sincerely and entirely to God will experience freely the full assurance of faith and all that the Word has promised. Our weakness of faith arises from duplicity of heart. The blood has so perfectly atoned for and conquered sin that nothing can hold the believer back from free admission to God.

Let us draw near, having our hearts sprinkled from an evil conscience and our bodies washed with pure water. Let us receive faith into our hearts in the perfect power of the blood, and let us forsake all that is not in accord with the purity of the Holy Place. Then we will begin to feel more at home in the Holiest Place. In Christ, who is our Life, *ye who at another time were far off are made near by the blood of the Christ* (Ephesians 2:13). Then we learn to carry on all our work in the Holiest. Everything we do is a spiritual sacrifice that pleases God in Jesus Christ.

The call to draw near has special reference to prayer – not as though we were not always in the Holiest, but some moments are more intimate, when the soul turns itself entirely to God to be engaged with Him alone. But our prayer is too often a calling out to God from a distance, so there is little power in it. *Let us draw near* with each prayer. Yes, let us take time to draw near and then pray. Then, we can lay our desires and wishes before our Father in the assurance that they are an acceptable incense. Then, prayer is a true *drawing near* to God, an exercise of inner fellowship with Him; then, we can have courage and power to carry on our work of intercession and to pray blessings on others. He who dwells in the Holy Place through the power of the blood is truly one of God's saints, and the power of God's presence goes out from him upon those who are around him.

Let us draw near, let us pray for ourselves, for one another, for everyone. May we abide in the sanctuary that we may carry the presence of our God with us everywhere. Let this be the fountain of life for us that grows from strength to strength and from glory to glory.

Chapter 8

Life in the Blood

Jesus said unto them, Verily, verily, I say unto you,
Unless ye eat the flesh of the Son of man and drink
his blood, ye shall have no life in you. Whosoever
eats my flesh and drinks my blood has eternal life,
and I will raise him up at the last day. For my flesh is
food indeed, and my blood is drink indeed. He that
eats my flesh and drinks my blood abides in me, and
I in him. The Spirit is he that gives life; the flesh prof-
its nothing; the words that I have spoken unto you,
they are Spirit and they are life. (John 6:53-56, 63)

The cup of blessing which we bless, is it not
the fellowship of the blood of the Christ?
(1 Corinthians 10:16)

The drinking of the blood of the Lord Jesus is the subject brought before us in these words. Just as water has a two-fold effect, so it is with this holy blood.

When water is used for washing, it cleanses; but if we drink it, we are refreshed and revived. He who desires to know the full power of the blood of Jesus must be taught by Him what the blessing of drinking the blood is. Everyone knows the difference between washing and drinking. Necessary and pleasant as it is to use water for cleansing, it is much more necessary and reviving to drink it. Without its cleansing, it is not possible to live as we ought, but without drinking, we cannot live at all. Only by drinking can we enjoy the full benefit of its power to sustain life.

Without drinking the blood of the Son of God – that is, without hearty appropriation of it – eternal life cannot be obtained.

To many people there is something unpleasant in the phrase *drinking the blood of the Son of man*, but it was more disagreeable to the Jews, for the use of blood was forbidden by the law of Moses under severe penalties. *For the soul of all flesh, its life, is in its blood; therefore, I have said unto the sons of Israel, Ye shall not eat the blood of any flesh, for the soul (or the life) of all flesh is its blood; whoever eats it shall be cut off* (Leviticus 17:14).

When Jesus spoke of drinking his blood, it naturally bothered them, because it was an unspeakable offence to their religious tradition. Our Lord would not have used the phrase if He had been able to make the deepest and most glorious truths concerning salvation by the blood plain to them and us any other way.

In seeking to become partakers of salvation, we must endeavor to understand three aspects:

1. The blessing in drinking the blood.

2. How this blessing is worked out in us.

3. Our attitude toward the drinking.

The Blessing in Drinking the Blood

We've seen that drinking expresses a more intimate connection with water than washing and therefore produces a more powerful effect. A blessing exists in the fellowship with the blood of Jesus that goes much further than cleansing or sanctification, and we can see how far the blessing indicated by this phrase reaches.

Not only must the blood do something for us by placing us in a new relationship with God, but it must also do something in us, entirely renewing us within. The words of the Lord Jesus draw our attention to this renewing when He says, *Unless ye eat the flesh of the Son of man and drink his blood, ye shall have no life in you* (John 6:53). Our Lord distinguishes two kinds of life. The Jews in His presence had a natural life of body and soul. Many among them were devout, well-intentioned men, but He said they had no life in them unless they ate His flesh and drank His blood. They needed another life, a new, heavenly life, which He possessed and which He could impart. All creature life must obtain nourishment outside of itself. The natural life was naturally nourished with bread and water. The heavenly life must be nourished with heavenly food and drink by Jesus Himself. *Unless ye eat the flesh of the Son of man and drink his blood, ye shall have no life in you.* Nothing less than His life must become ours – the life that He, as the Son of Man, lived on earth.

Our Lord emphasized this more strongly in words that follow, in which He again explained what the nature of that life is: *Whosoever eats my flesh and drinks my blood has eternal life, and I will raise him up at the last day* (John 6:54). Eternal life is the life of God. Our Lord came to earth the first time to reveal that eternal life in the flesh and then to communicate it to us who are in the flesh. In Him we see the eternal life dwelling in its divine power in a body of flesh, which was taken up into heaven. He tells us that those who eat His flesh and drink His blood, who partake of His body as their sustenance, will experience the power of eternal life in their own bodies. *I will raise him up at the last day* (John 6:54). The marvel of the eternal life in Christ is that it was eternal life in a human body. We must be partakers of that body, and then our body, possessing that life, will one day be raised from the dead.

Our Lord said, *My flesh is food indeed, and my blood is drink indeed* (John 6:55). The word translated *indeed* here is the same as the one He used when He spoke His parable of the true Vine, *I AM the true* [the indeed] *vine*, thus indicating the difference between what was only a symbol and what is actual truth (John 15:1). Earthly food is not real food, for it does not impart real life. The one true food is the body and blood of the Lord Jesus Christ, which imparts and sustains life, and not merely as a shadow or in a symbolic manner. No, this word indicates that in a full and real sense the flesh and blood of the Lord Jesus are the food by which eternal life is nourished and sustained in us: *My flesh is food indeed, and my blood is drink indeed.*

In order to point out the reality and power of this food, our Lord added, *He that eats my flesh and drinks my blood abides in me, and I in him* (John 6:56). Nourishment by His flesh and blood effects the most perfect union with Him. This is the reason that His flesh and blood have the power of eternal life. Our Lord declares here that those who believe in Him are to experience not only certain influences from Him in their hearts but are also to be brought into the closest abiding union with Him.

This then is the blessing of drinking the blood of the Son of Man – becoming one with Him, becoming a partaker of the divine nature in Him. How real this union is may be seen from the words which follow: *As . . . I live by the Father, so he that eats me, he shall also live by me* (John 6:57). Nothing, except the union that exists between our Lord and the Father, can serve as a type of our union with Him. Just as in the invisible, divine nature, the two Persons are truly One, so man becomes one with Jesus; the union is as real as that in the divine nature, with one difference: as human nature cannot exist apart from the body, this union includes the body also.

Our Lord prepared for Himself a body into which He took up a human body. By the body and blood of Jesus, this body became a sharer in eternal life, in the life of our Lord Himself. Those who desire to receive the fullness of this blessing must be careful to enjoy all that the Scripture offers them in the holy, mysterious expression to drink the blood of Christ.

How This Blessing Is Worked Out in Us

The first idea that presents itself here is that drinking indicates the deep, true appropriation in our spirit by faith of all we understand concerning the power of the blood.

We speak sometimes of *drinking in* the words of a speaker, when we heartily give ourselves up to listen and receive them. So when anyone's heart is filled with a sense of the preciousness and power of the blood, when he is lost in the contemplation of it with real joy, when he takes it for himself and seeks confirmation of the life-giving power of that blood, then it may be said that he drinks the blood of Jesus. He absorbs into the depths of his soul all that faith enables him to see of redemption, cleansing, and sanctification by the blood.

There is a deep truth in this representation, and it gives us a very glorious demonstration of the way in which the full blessing by the blood may be obtained. And yet it is certain that our Lord intended something more than this by so repeatedly making use of the expression of eating his flesh and drinking his blood. What this further truth is becomes clear by his institution of the Lord's Supper. For, although our Savior did not actually deal with that Supper when He taught in Capernaum, He spoke of it later at the Last Supper.

In the Reformed Churches, there are two views regarding the Lord's Supper. According to one, which is named after the reformer Zwingli, the bread and wine are merely tokens or representations of a spiritual truth. They are meant to teach us that as sure as bread and wine, when eaten or drunk, nourish and revive, even more surely the body and blood, recognized and appropriated by faith, nourish and quicken the soul.

According to the other view, which bears the name of Calvin, there is something more than this in the eating of the Supper. He teaches that in a hidden and incomprehensible way through the Holy Spirit, we become so nourished by the body and blood of Jesus in heaven that even our body, through the power of His body, becomes a partaker in the power of eternal life. In this way, he connects the resurrection of the body with the eating of Christ's body in the Lord's Supper. He writes thus:

The bodily presence which the Sacrament demands is such, and exercises such a power here (in the Supper) that it becomes not only the undoubted assurance in our spirit of eternal life, but also assures the immortality of the flesh. If anyone asks me how this can be, I am not ashamed to acknowledge that it is a mystery too high for my spirit to comprehend, or my words to express. I feel it more than I can understand it. It may seem incredible indeed that the flesh of Christ should reach us from such immense local distance so as to become our food. But we must remember how far the power of the Holy Spirit transcends all our senses. Let faith then embrace what the understanding cannot grasp; namely, the sacred communication of His flesh and blood by which Christ transfuses His life into us, just as if it penetrated our bones and marrow.

The communion of the flesh and blood of Christ is necessary for all who desire to inherit eternal life. The apostle refers to *the congregation* [church], *which is his body* (Ephesians 1:22-23). Later, Paul refers to Christ as the head and our bodies as the members of Christ (Ephesians 4:15; 1 Corinthians 6:15). We see that all of this cannot take place if He is not attached to us in body and spirit. The apostle Paul again makes use of a glorious expression, *We are members of his body, of his flesh, and of his bones* (Ephesians 5:30). Then He cries out, *This is a great mystery* (Ephesians 5:32). It would therefore be foolish not to recognize the communion of believers in the body and blood of the Lord – a communion that the apostle esteemed so great that he wondered at it, rather than explained it.

There is something more in the Lord's Supper than simply the believer appropriating the redemptive work of Christ. This is made clear in the Heidelberg catechism in Question 76: "What does it then mean to eat the crucified body of Christ and to drink His shed blood?"[4] The answer is, "It is not only to embrace with a believing heart all the sufferings and death of Christ and receive pardon of sin and eternal life, but also to become more united to His sacred body by the Holy Spirit who dwells both in Christ and in us. So, though Christ is in heaven and we are on earth, we are flesh of His flesh and bone of His bones, and we live and are governed for ever by one Spirit."[5]

The thoughts that are expressed in this teaching are in entire agreement with Scripture. In the creation of man, the remarkable thing that should distinguish him from the spirits, which God had previously created and which should make man the crowning work of God's wisdom and power, was that he should reveal the life of the spirit and the glory of God in a body formed out of dust. Through the body, lust and sin came into the world. Full redemption is designed to deliver the body and to make it God's abode. *For since by a man came death, by a man came also the resurrection of the dead. For as in Adam all die, even*

4   When we speak of eating the body, we are not speaking of eating a physical body but believing in the finished work of our Lord. The wording in this question itself (the crucified body) tends to suggest a more physical meaning. It is important to note that when referring to Christ's body that we share, it is never referred to the crucified body in Scripture.

5   PUBLISHER'S NOTE: It is our belief that the sacraments don't in reality become part of the physical body of Christ. Instead, it appears that scripture tells us that we are to *do this in remembrance of Jesus Christ* (1 Corinthians 11:23-26)

so in the Christ shall all be made alive (1 Corinthians 15:21-22). Redemption will be perfect and God's purpose accomplished only then. This was the purpose for which the Lord Jesus came in the flesh, and in Him dwelt *all the fullness of the Godhead bodily* (Colossians 2:9). For this He bore our sins in His body on the tree, and by His death and resurrection He delivered the body as well as the spirit from the power of sin and death.

As the firstfruits of this redemption, we are now one body, as well as one Spirit, with Him. We are of His body, of His flesh, and of His bones. It is because of this that in the observance of the Lord's Supper, the Lord comes to the body and takes possession of it. Not only does He work by His Spirit on our spirit to make our body share in redemption at the resurrection. No, the body is also the temple of the Spirit, and the sanctification of soul and spirit will progress more gloriously in proportion as the undivided personality, including the body, which exercises such an opposing influence, has a share in it.

Thus, in the sacrament we are intentionally fed by the real natural body and the real blood of Christ. We do not follow the teaching of Luther that the body of Christ is so in the bread that even an unbeliever who eats the holy body receives the power of the holy body and blood from heaven and becomes a partaker of eternal life.

All that has now been said about the Lord's Supper must have its full application to the drinking of the blood of Jesus. It is a deep spiritual mystery in which the most intimate, the most perfect union with Christ, is effected. It takes place where through the Holy Spirit, the soul fully appropriates the communion of the blood of Christ and becomes a true partaker of the disposition which He revealed in the shedding of His blood. The blood is the soul, the life of the body, where the believer as one body with Christ desires to abide perfectly in Him. Through the Spirit in a superhuman powerful way, the blood will support and strengthen the heavenly life. The life that was poured out becomes his life. The life of the old "I" dies to make room for the life of Christ in him. By perceiving how this drinking is the highest participation in the heavenly life of the Lord, faith has one of its highest and most glorious offices.

Our Attitude toward the Drinking

Beloved brethren, you have already heard that this is one of the deepest mysteries of the life of God in us. It behooves us to draw near with deep reverence while we ask the Lord Jesus to teach us what He means by drinking His blood.

Only those who long for a full union with Jesus will understand what it is to drink the blood of Jesus. *He that eats my flesh and drinks my blood abides in me, and I in him* (John 6:56). He who is satisfied with just the forgiveness of his sins and does not thirst to drink abundantly of the love of Jesus will miss many blessings. If he does not desire to experience redemption for soul and body in its full power to acquire the same disposition that was in Jesus, he will only have a small share in the benefits offered through the blood. On the other hand, if his chief objective is also the object of Jesus, and he desires that the power of eternal life should operate in his body, he will be concerned that these words are too high or too mysterious. He longs to become heavenly minded because he belongs to heaven; therefore, he desires to also obtain his meat and drink from heaven. Without thirst, there is no drinking. The longing after Jesus and perfect fellowship with Him is the thirst that is the best preparation for drinking the blood.

It is by the Holy Spirit that the thirsty soul will drink of the heavenly refreshment of this life-giving drink. This drinking is a heavenly mystery. In heaven, where God the Judge and Jesus the Mediator of the new covenant abide, there is *the blood of sprinkling* (Hebrews 12:23-24). When the Holy Spirit teaches us,

He bestows more than our human understanding can grasp. All the thoughts that we can entertain about the blood or the life of Jesus and our share in that blood as members of His body and the impartation of the living power of that blood are but feeble rays of the glorious reality, which the Holy Spirit will bring to fruition in us through our union with Jesus.

Where in our human bodies do we find that the blood is actually received? Isn't it where one member of the body after another receives the blood stream, which is continually renewed from the heart? Each member of a healthy body ceaselessly and abundantly drinks in the blood. So the Spirit of Life in Christ Jesus who unites us to Him will make this drinking of the blood the natural action of the inner life. When the Jews complained that what the Lord had spoken concerning eating His flesh and drinking His blood was *a hard word*, He said, *the Spirit is he that gives life; the flesh profits nothing* (John 6:63). It is the Holy Spirit who makes this divine mystery life and power in us – a true living experience, in which we abide in Jesus and He in us.

On our part, we must have a quiet, strong, settled expectancy of faith that this blessing will be granted to us. We must believe that all that the precious blood can do, or bestow, is for us.

Let us believe that through the Holy Spirit the Savior Himself will cause us to drink His blood unto life. Let us believe and appropriate those effects of the blood, which we understand – namely, its reconciling, cleansing, and sanctifying effects.

We may then say to the Lord, "O Lord, Your blood is my life drink. You who have washed and cleansed me by that blood, You will teach me every day to eat the flesh of the Son of Man and to drink His blood, so that I may abide in You and You in me." He will surely do this.

Chapter 9

Victory through the Blood

*They have overcome him by the blood of the Lamb
and by the word of their testimony; and they loved
not their lives unto the death.* (Revelation 12:11)

For thousands of years there had been a mighty conflict between the old Serpent, who led man astray, and the seed of the woman for possession of mankind. *And the LORD God said unto the serpent, Because thou hast done this, thou art cursed above all beasts and above every animal of the field; upon thy belly shalt thou go, and dust shalt thou eat all the days of thy life; and I will put enmity between thee and the woman and between thy seed and her seed; that seed shall bruise thy head, and thou shalt bruise his heel* (Genesis 3:14-15).

Often it seemed as though the kingdom of God had come into power; then at other times the might of evil obtained such supremacy that the strife appeared to be hopeless.

The life of our Lord Jesus was the same. By His coming with His wonderful words and works, the most glorious expectations of a speedy redemption were awakened. The disappointment, which the death of Jesus brought to all who had believed in

Him, was terrible. It seemed, indeed, as if the powers of darkness had conquered and had established their kingdom forever.

But, Jesus is risen from the dead, an apparent victory that proved to be the terrible downfall of the Prince of Darkness. By bringing about the death of the Lord of life, Satan permitted Him, who alone was able to break open the gates of death, to enter his kingdom. *He also himself likewise took part of the same, that through death he might destroy him that had the empire of death, that is, the devil* (Hebrews 2:14). In that holy moment when our Lord shed His blood in death, and it seemed as if Satan was victorious, the adversary was robbed of the authority he had thus far possessed.

Our text gives a grand representation of these memorable events. The best commentators, in spite of differences in details, are united in thinking that we have in Revelation 12 and 20 a vision of the casting out of Satan from heaven as a result of the ascension of Christ.

We read in Revelation 12:5, 7-9: The woman *brought forth a man child, who . . . was caught up unto God and to his throne. And there was war in heaven: Michael and his angels fought against the dragon; and the dragon fought and his angels, and did not prevail; neither was their place found any more in heaven. And the great dragon was cast out, the serpent of old, who is called the Devil and Satan, who deceives the whole world; he was cast out into the earth, and his angels were cast out with him.*

Then follows the song from which the text is taken: *Now is come salvation and virtue and the kingdom of our God and the power of his Christ; for the accuser of our brethren is cast down, who accused them before our God day and night. And they have overcome him by the blood of the Lamb and by the word of their testimony; and they loved not their lives unto the death. Therefore, rejoice, ye heavens, and ye that dwell in them* (Revelation 12:10-12).

The point which deserves our special attention is that while the conquest of Satan and his being cast out of heaven is first represented as the result of the ascension of Jesus and the war in heaven, in the song of triumph which was heard in heaven, victory is ascribed chiefly to the blood of the Lamb. This was the power by which the victory was gained.

Through the whole book of Revelation, we see the Lamb on the throne. He has gained that position because He was slain; the victory over Satan and all his authority is by the blood of the Lamb.

We have looked at the manifold effects of the blood, but it is fitting to understand how that victory is always ascribed to the blood of the Lamb.

We shall consider victory:

1. Victory – once for all.

2. Victory – ongoing and progressive.

3. Victory – shared.

Victory – Once for All

In the picture given in our text, we see what a high position Satan, the great Enemy of the human race, once occupied. He had entrance into heaven and appeared there as the accuser of the saints and as the opponent of whatever was done in the interests of God's people.

We know how this is taught in the Old Testament. In the book of Job, we see Satan coming with the sons of God to present himself before the Lord and obtain permission from Him to tempt His servant Job:

> *Then Satan answered the LORD and said, Does Job fear God for nothing? Hast thou not made a hedge about him and about his house and about all that he has on every side? Thou hast blessed the work of*

*his hands; therefore, his substance has increased in
the land. But put forth thy hand now and touch all
that he has, and thou shalt see if he will not blas-
pheme thee to thy face. And the LORD said to Satan,
Behold, all that he has is in thy power; only upon
himself do not put forth thy hand. So Satan went
forth from the presence of the LORD* (Job 1:9-12).

In Zechariah 3:1 we read that he saw *Joshua the high priest,
standing before the angel of the LORD, and Satan standing at
his right hand to resist him.* The English Revised Version says
Satan stood *at his right hand to be his adversary.*

Then in the book of Luke, our Lord states: *I beheld Satan
as lightning fall from heaven* (Luke 10:18). Later, in His agony
of soul as He anticipated His sufferings, He said, *Now is the
judgment of this world; now shall the prince of this world be
cast out* (John 12:31).

It may seem strange that the Scriptures should represent
Satan as being in heaven, but to understand this correctly,
we must remember that heaven is not a small dwelling place
where God and Satan had communication as neighbors. No,
heaven is an endless sphere with many different divisions,
filled with innumerable hosts of angels who carry out God's
will in nature. Among them, Satan still held a place. We must
also remember that he is not represented in Scripture to be the
black, grisly figure as he is generally pictured, but rather as an
angel of light (2 Corinthians 11:14). He was a prince with ten
thousands of servants.

When he had brought about the fall of man, he transferred
the world to himself and became its prince; he had real authority
over all that was in it. Man had been destined to be king of this
world, for *God said unto them, . . . fill the earth and subdue it and
have dominion over* it (Genesis 1:28). When Satan conquered
the king, he took his entire kingdom under his authority, and

this authority was recognized by God. In His holy will, God had ordained that if man listened to Satan, he must suffer the consequences and become subject to his tyranny. God never abused His power or exercised force by doing this but always acted out of His righteousness. So Satan retained his authority until it was taken from him in a lawful manner.

This is why he could appear before God in heaven as the accuser of the saints and in opposition to them for the four thousand years of the old covenant. He had obtained authority over all flesh, and only after he was conquered in flesh, as the sphere of his authority, could he be cast out forever as the accuser from heaven. So the Son of God had to come in the flesh to fight and conquer Satan on his own ground.

For this reason also, after our Lord was recognized as the Son of God, He *was led up of the Spirit into the wilderness to be tempted by the devil* (Matthew 4:1). Victory over Satan could be gained only after He had personally endured and resisted his temptations.

But even this victory was not sufficient. Christ came in order that *through death he might destroy him that had the empire of death, that is, the devil* (Hebrews 2:14). The devil had that power of death because of the law of God. That law had installed him as jailer of its prisoners. Scripture says, *The sting of death is sin, and the power of sin is the law* (1 Corinthians 15:56). Victory over and the casting out of Satan could not take place until the righteous demands of the law were perfectly fulfilled. The sinner must be delivered from the power of the law before he could be delivered from the authority of Satan.

It was through His death and the shedding of His blood that the Lord Jesus fulfilled the law's demands. Ceaselessly, the law had been declaring that *the wages of sin is death* and *the soul that sins, it shall die* (Romans 6:23; Ezekiel 18:20). By the ministry of the temple and the sacrifices with the shedding and sprinkling of blood, the Law had foretold that reconciliation and redemption could take place only by the shedding of blood.

As our security, the Son of God was born under the law. He obeyed it perfectly. He resisted the temptations of Satan to withdraw Himself from under its authority. He willingly gave Himself up to bear the punishment of sin. He would not listen to the temptation of Satan to refuse the cup of suffering. When He shed His blood, He had devoted His whole life to the fulfilling of the law. When the law had been perfectly fulfilled, the authority of sin and Satan was brought to an end. Therefore, death could not hold Him. *Through the blood of the eternal testament*, God brought Him *again from the dead* (Hebrews 13:20). So also *by his own blood he entered in once into the sanctuary designed for eternal redemption* to make His reconciliation effective for us (Hebrews 9:12).

The text gives us a striking description of the glorious result of the appearing of our Lord in heaven. Concerning the mystic woman, we read: *She brought forth a man child, who was to rule all the Gentiles with a rod of iron; and her child was caught up unto God and to his throne. And there was war in heaven: Michael and his angels fought against the dragon; and the dragon fought and his angels, and did not prevail; neither was their place found any more in heaven. And the great dragon was cast out, the serpent of old, who is called the Devil and Satan, who deceives the whole world; he was cast out into the earth, and his angels were cast out with him* (Revelation 12:5, 7-9). Then follows the song of victory with the words of our text: *They have overcome him by the blood of the Lamb* (Revelation 12:11).

In the book of Daniel, we read of a previous conflict between this Michael, who stood on the side of God's people Israel, and the opposing world powers. But only in Revelation can Satan be cast out, because of the blood of the Lamb. Reconciliation for sin and the fulfilment of the law have taken all his authority and rights from him. The blood that had done such wonderful things in heaven in blotting out sin and bringing it to nothing had a similar power over Satan. Now he has no right to accuse. *Now is come salvation and virtue and the kingdom of our God and the power of his Christ; for the accuser of our brethren is cast down, . . . And they have overcome him by the blood of the Lamb* (Revelation 12:10-11).

Victory – Ongoing and Progressive

Satan has been cast down to earth, so the heavenly victory must now be carried out here. This is indicated in the words of the song of victory, *They have overcome him by the blood of the Lamb.* This was primarily spoken concerning the brethren mentioned, but it refers also to the victory of the angels. The victory in heaven and on earth progresses simultaneously and rests on the same ground.

We know from Daniel what fellowship there exists between heaven and earth in carrying on the work of God:

> *And he said unto me, Fear not, Daniel: for from the first day that thou didst give thy heart to understand and to afflict thy soul before thy God, thy words were heard, and I am come because of thy words. But the prince of the kingdom of Persia withstood me twenty-one days: and behold, Michael, one of the chief princes, came to help me; and I remained there with the kings of Persia.* (Daniel 10:12-13)

As soon as Daniel prayed, the angel became active, and the three weeks' battle in the heavenlies were three weeks of prayer and fasting on earth. The conflict here on earth is the result of a conflict in the invisible region of the heavenlies. Michael and his angels, as well as the brethren on earth, gained the victory by the blood of the Lamb.

In the twelfth chapter of Revelation, we see how the conflict was removed from heaven to earth. *Woe to the inhabiters of the earth*, exclaimed the voice in heaven, *for the devil is come down unto you, having great wrath, knowing that he has but a short time. And when the dragon saw that he was cast unto the earth, he persecuted the woman who brought forth the man child* (Revelation 12:12-13).

The woman signifies nothing but the church of God out of which Jesus was born. When the devil could not harm Him anymore, he persecuted His church. The disciples of our Lord and the church in the first three centuries had experienced this. In the bloody persecutions where hundreds of thousands of Christians perished as martyrs, Satan did his utmost to lead the church into apostasy or to root it out altogether. In its full sense, the statement that *they have overcome him by the blood of the Lamb and by the word of their testimony; and they loved not their lives unto the death* applies to the martyrs.

After centuries of persecution came centuries of rest and worldly prosperity. In vain, Satan had tried force, but by winning the favor of the world, he might have better success. Conformed to the world, everything in the church became darker and darker, until the Roman apostasy reached its climax in the Middle Ages. Nevertheless, during all these ages many fought the fight of faith in the midst of surrounding misery. By their reverence and witness for the Lord, the statement was often established: *They have overcome him by the blood of the Lamb and by the word of their testimony; and they loved not their lives unto the death.*

Satan's authority was broken down by this secret power through the blessed Reformation. *They have overcome him by the blood of the Lamb.* The discovery, experience, and preaching of the glorious truth that we are *justified freely by his grace through the redemption that is in Jesus, the Christ, whom God purposed for reconciliation through faith in his blood* gave the reformers such wonderful power and glorious victory (Romans 3:24-25).

Since the days of the Reformation, the church has been inspired by a new life to obtain victory over deadness in proportion to how the blood of the Lamb is glorified. Yes, even in the midst of the wildest heathen where the throne of Satan has been undisturbed for thousands of years, the blood of the Lamb is still the weapon to destroy Satan's power. The preaching of the blood of the cross as the reconciliation for the sin of the world and the basis for God's free, forgiving love is the power by which the most darkened heart is opened and softened. That heart is transformed from being a dwelling place of Satan to a temple of the Most High.

This provision for the church is also available for each Christian. In *the blood of the Lamb,* he always has victory. When the soul is convinced of the power of that blood to effect a perfect reconciliation and the blotting out of sin, it robs the devil of his authority over us and works in our hearts a full assurance of the favor of God. When the soul lives in the power of the blood to destroy the power of sin, the temptations of Satan cease to ensnare the individual.

God dwells where the holy blood of the Lamb is applied, and Satan is put to flight. In heaven, on earth, and in our hearts the blood of the Lamb provides an ongoing victory. *They have overcome him by the blood of the Lamb.*

Victory – Shared

If we are counted with those who have been cleansed in the blood of the Lamb, we also share in the victory. To have the full enjoyment of this, however, we must understand the following facts:

No Victory Without Conflict
We must recognize that we dwell in the Enemy's territory. What was revealed to the apostle in his heavenly vision must hold

true in our daily lives. Satan has been cast down to the earth and has great wrath because his time is short. He cannot reach the glorified Jesus now but seeks to reach Him by attacking His people. We must live under the consciousness that every moment we are watched by an Enemy with unimaginable cunning and power. He does not tire in his endeavor to bring us under his authority. He is literally *the prince of this world* (John 14:30). All that is in the world is ready to serve him, and he knows how to make use of it in his attempts to lead the church to be unfaithful to her Lord and to inspire her with his spirit – the spirit of the world.

He not only uses temptations that are commonly esteemed to be sin, but he also knows how to gain an entrance into our earthly engagements and businesses. He seeks to influence in our daily bread, financial affairs, and politics. He tries to control our literature, science, and knowledge; in all things, he works to turn all that is lawful in itself into a tool for his devilish deceptions.

The believer who desires to share in the victory over Satan through the blood of the Lamb must be a fighter. He must understand the character of his Enemy. He must allow himself to be taught by the Spirit through the Word what the secret cunning of Satan is by which he so often blinds and deceives men. The believer must know that this battle is *not against flesh and blood, but against principalities, against powers, against the lords of this age, rulers of this darkness, against spiritual wickedness in the heavens* (Ephesians 6:12). He must devote himself to carrying on the conflict until death. Only then will he be able to join in the song of victory, *They have overcome him by the blood of the Lamb and by the word of their testimony; and they loved not their lives unto the death.*

Victory Through Faith

This is the victory that overcomes the world, even our faith. *Who is he that overcomes the world, but he that believes that Jesus is the Son of God?* (1 John 5:4-5). *Be of good cheer,* said our Lord Jesus; *I have overcome the world.* Satan is already a conquered enemy. He has nothing to say to one who belongs to the Lord Jesus.

By unbelief, ignorance, or doubting my assurance in the victory of Jesus, I may give Satan an authority over me, which otherwise he does not possess. But when I know that I am one with the Lord Jesus and that He lives in me and maintains that victory which He gained, then Satan has no power over me. Victory through the blood of the Lamb is the power of my life.

Only this faith can inspire courage and joy in the battle. By thinking of the terrible power of the Enemy, his never-sleeping watchfulness, and the way he has taken possession of everything on earth to tempt us, it might be said that the battle is too severe, or it is not possible to live always under such tension, or that life is impossible. This is perfectly true if we had to meet the Enemy in our weakness or gain the victory by our own might. But that is not what we are called upon to do. Jesus is the Victor, so we only need to have our souls filled with the heavenly vision of Satan being cast out of heaven by Jesus. Our souls need to be filled with faith in the blood by which Jesus Himself conquered and with faith that He Himself is with us to maintain the power and victory of His blood. Then *we are more than conquerors through him that loved us* (Romans 8:37).

Victory in Fellowship with the Blood

Faith is not merely a thought I grasp or a conviction that possesses me; it is a life. Faith brings the soul into direct contact with God and the unseen things of heaven, but above all, with the blood of Jesus. To believe in victory over Satan is not possible without putting myself under the power of the blood.

Belief in the power of the blood produces in me a desire for an experience of its power; each experience of its power makes belief in victory more glorious.

Seek to enter more deeply into the perfect reconciliation with God, which is yours. Live by constantly exercising faith in the assurance that the blood cleanses from all sin and yield yourself to be sanctified and brought near to God through the blood; let it be your life-giving nourishment and power. You will thus have an unbroken experience of victory over Satan and his temptations. He who walks with God will rule as a conquering king over Satan.

Believers, our Lord Jesus has made us not only priests but also kings unto God that we may draw near to Him and rule for Him. A kingly spirit must inspire us – a kingly courage to rule over our enemies. The blood of the Lamb must be a token and a seal, not only of reconciliation for all guilt but also of victory over all the power of sin.

The resurrection and ascension of Jesus and the casting out of Satan were the results of the shedding of His blood. The sprinkling of the blood will open our way for the full enjoyment of resurrection with Jesus and being seated with Him in the heavenly places.

Therefore, once again, I beseech you to open your entire being to the incoming of the power of the blood of Jesus; then your life will become a continual observance of the resurrection and ascension of our Lord and a continual victory over all the powers of hell. Your heart will constantly unite with the song of heaven, *Now is come salvation and virtue and the kingdom of our God and the power of his Christ; for the accuser of our brethren is cast down, . . . they have overcome him by the blood of the Lamb* (Revelation 12:10-11).

Chapter 10

Heavenly Joy Through the Blood

After this I saw, and, behold, a great multitude,
which no man could number, . . . stood before the
throne and before the Lamb . . . and cried with a loud
voice, saying, Salvation unto him who is seated upon
the throne of our God and unto the Lamb. These are
those who came out of great tribulation and have
washed their long robes, and made them white in the
blood of the Lamb. (Revelation 7:9-10, 14)

These words occur in the well-known vision of the great
multitude in heavenly glory, which no man could number.
In spirit, the apostle saw them standing before the throne of
God and of the Lamb; they were clothed with long, white robes
and held palms in their hands. They sang with a loud voice,
Salvation unto him who is seated upon the throne of our God
and unto the Lamb (Revelation 7:10). All the angels answered
this song by falling down on their faces before the throne to
worship God and offer eternal praise and glory to Him.

Then one of the elders, pointing out the great multitude and
the clothing that distinguished them, put the question to John,

Who are these who are arrayed in long white robes? and where did they come from? (Revelation 7:13)

John replied, *lord, thou knowest.*

Then the elder said, *These are those who came out of great tribulation and have washed their long robes, and made them white in the blood of the Lamb. Therefore, they are before the throne of God and serve him day and night in his temple* (Revelation 7:14-15).

This explanation, concerning the state of the redeemed in their heavenly glory and given by one of the elders who stood around the throne, is of great value. It reveals to us that not only in this world of sin and strife is the blood of Jesus the one hope of the sinner, but that in heaven when every enemy has been subdued, that precious blood will also be recognized forever as the basis of our salvation. And we learn that the blood must exercise its power with God in heaven. Not only does the blood still have to deal with sin on earth, but for all eternity it will also bear the sign that the redeemed owes his salvation entirely to it.

If we understand this better, we will experience a true and vital connection between the sprinkling of the blood and the joys of heaven. A true, intimate connection with the blood on earth will enable the believer to share the joy and glory of heaven while on earth.

The blood causes joy in heaven because it:

1. Grants the right to a place in heaven.

2. Makes us fit for the pleasures of heaven.

3. Provides details for the song of heaven.

A Place in Heaven

It is clear that this is the main thought in the text. In the question,

Who are these who are arrayed in long white robes? and where did they come from? The elder desires to bring attention and inquiry to who these favored persons are who stand before the throne and before the Lamb with palms in their hands. And, as he gives the reply, we expect that he will mention what might be the most remarkable thing in their appearance. He replies to the question, *Where did they come from?* by saying that they *came out of great tribulation.* To the question, *Who are these?* he replies that they are those who *have washed their long robes, and made them white in the blood of the Lamb.*

That is the one thing the elder draws attention to as their distinguishing mark. This alone gives them the right to the place which they occupy in glory. This becomes evident, if we notice the words which immediately follow: *Therefore, they are before the throne of God and serve him day and night in his temple, and he that is seated on the throne shall dwell among them. Therefore* – it is because of that blood that they are before the throne. They owe their place in glory to the blood of the Lamb. The blood gives them the right to heaven.

A right to heaven! Can such a thing be spoken of in connection with a condemned sinner? Wouldn't it be better to only glory in the mercy of God who, by free grace, admits a sinner to heaven, than to speak of a right to heaven? No, it would not be better, for then we would not understand the value of the blood or why it had to be shed. We might also entertain false conceptions both of our sin and of God's grace and remain unfit for the full enjoyment of the glorious redemption which the Savior has accomplished for us.

We have already considered that Satan *was cast out into the earth* from heaven, and we see from this incident that a holy God always acts according to law. Just as the devil was not *cast out* except according to law and right, so the sinner cannot be admitted in any other way. The prophet Isaiah said, *Zion shall be ransomed with judgment and her converts with righteousness* (Isaiah 1:27). The apostle Paul tells us that *as sin has reigned unto death, even so might grace reign through righteousness unto eternal life* (Romans 5:21). This was the reason God sent His Son into the world. Instead of being afraid that speaking of having a right to enter heaven might belittle grace, it will be acknowledged that the highest glory of grace consists in granting that right.

The lack of this insight is sometimes found in the church where it might be least expected. Recently I asked a man, who spoke of the hope he had of going to heaven when he died, what he rested his hope on. He was not by any means a careless man, nor did he trust in his own righteousness, but he replied, "Well, I think that I strive to seek the Lord and to do His will." When I told him that this was no ground to stand on before the judgment seat of a holy God, he appealed to the mercy of God. When I told him, again, that he needed more than mercy, he did not seem to have heard or understood that it was the righteousness of God alone that could grant him entrance into heaven. I fear there are many who listen to the preaching of justification by faith, but who have no idea that they cannot have a share in eternal blessedness except by being declared legally righteous.

Entirely different was the testimony of a young man who was learning-disabled, but whose heart the Spirit of God had enlightened to understand the meaning of the crucifixion of Jesus.

When on his deathbed, he was asked about his hope for eternity, he intimated that there was a great book; on one of the pages of this book his many sins had been written. Then, with the finger of his right hand, he pointed to the palm of his left hand, indicating the print of the nail there. Figuratively taking something from the pierced hand – he was thinking of the blood that marked it – he showed how all that was written on that page was now blotted out. The blood of the Lamb was the reason for his hope.

The blood of the Lamb gives the believing sinner a right to heaven; *Behold the Lamb of God, who takes away the sin of the world* (John 1:29). By shedding His blood, He bore the punishment of sin. He gave Himself up to death in our place. He gave His life as a ransom for many. Now our Lord's blood has really been shed as a ransom for us, as punishment for our sin. Now the righteousness of God declares that the blood fulfilled all the requirements of the law concerning punishment and obedience. God pronounces the sinner who believes in Christ to be righteous. Faith is just the recognition that Christ has done everything for me, and God's declaration of righteousness is just His declaration that according to the law and right, I have a title to salvation. God's grace grants me the right to heaven. The blood of the Lamb is the evidence of this right. If I have been cleansed by that blood, I can meet death with full confidence because I have a right to heaven.

You desire and hope to get to heaven. Listen to the answer given to the question, Who are they who will find a place before the throne of God? *These are those who came out of great tribulation and have washed their long robes, and made them white in the blood of the Lamb.* That washing doesn't take place in heaven or at death, but here during our life on earth. Do not deceive yourselves by a hope of heaven if you have not been cleansed by that precious blood. Do not dare to meet death without knowing that Jesus Himself has cleansed you by His blood.

Fit for the Pleasures of Heaven

It is of little use for men to have a right to anything unless they are fit to enjoy it. However costly the gift, it is of little use if the inner temperament necessary to enjoy it is lacking. To grant the right to heaven to those who are not prepared for it would give them no pleasure, but would be in conflict with the perfection of all God's works.

The power of the blood of Jesus not only opens heaven for the sinner, but it also works on him in such a divine way that as he enters heaven, it will appear that the blessedness of heaven and him have been fitted for each other.

Words of our text tell us what constitutes the blessedness of heaven and what disposition is necessary for it. *Therefore, they are before the throne of God and serve him day and night in his temple, and he that is seated on the throne shall dwell among them. They shall hunger no more neither thirst anymore; neither shall the sun be thrust upon them nor any other heat. For the Lamb which is in the midst of the throne shall govern them and shall lead them unto living fountains of waters, and God shall wipe away all tears from their eyes* (Revelation 7:15-16).

Nearness to and fellowship with God and the Lamb constitute the blessedness of heaven. To be before the throne of God and see His face, to serve Him day and night in His temple and be overshadowed by Him who sits upon the throne to be fed and led by the Lamb – all these expressions point out how little the blessedness of heaven depends on anything besides God and the Lamb. To see them and communicate with them, to be acknowledged, loved, and cared for by them – that is blessedness.

Two things are needed to prepare for such intimacy with God and the Lamb:

Inner agreement in mind and will
Delight in His nearness and fellowship

Inner Agreement
No thought for heaven is possible apart from oneness with God's will. How could two dwell together unless they agree? And because God is the Holy One, the sinner must be cleansed

from his sin and sanctified; otherwise, he remains utterly unfit for what constitutes the happiness of heaven. *Follow peace with everyone and holiness, without which no one shall see the Lord* (Hebrews 12:14). Man's entire nature must be renewed, so he can think, desire, will, and do what pleases God – not as a matter of mere obedience in keeping a commandment but from natural pleasure, and because he cannot do or will otherwise. Holiness must become his nature.

Isn't this what we have seen that the blood of the Lamb does? *The blood of Jesus Christ, his Son cleanses us from all sin* (1 John 1:7). Where reconciliation and pardon are applied by the Holy Spirit and retained by a living faith, the blood operates with a divine power, killing sinful lusts and desires; the blood constantly exercises a wonderful cleansing power. In the blood, the power of the death of Jesus operates; we died to sin with Him. Through a believing intimacy with the blood, the power of the death of Jesus presses into the innermost parts of our hidden life. The blood breaks the power of sin and cleanses us from all sin.

The blood also sanctifies. We have seen that cleansing is just one part of salvation, the taking away of sin. The blood does more than this; it takes possession of us for God and inwardly grants the same perspective which was in Jesus when He shed His blood. In shedding that blood, He sanctified Himself for us that we also could be sanctified by the truth. As we delight and lose ourselves in that holy blood, the power of entire surrender to God's will and glory, the power to sacrifice everything and abide in God's love, which inspired the Lord Jesus, is effective in us.

The blood sanctifies us for the emptying and surrender of ourselves, so that God may take possession of us and fill us with Himself. This is true holiness – to be possessed by and filled with God. This is worked out by the blood of the Lamb, so we are prepared here on earth to meet God in heaven with unspeakable joy.

Delight in His Nearness

In addition to having one will with God, fitness for heaven consists in the desire and capacity for enjoying fellowship with God. Here on earth, the blood imparts the true preparation for heaven. We have seen how the blood brings us near to God; we have liberty by the blood to enter into the Holiest of God's presence and make our dwelling place there. We have seen that God attaches such incomprehensible value to the blood that where the blood is sprinkled, there is His throne of grace. When a heart places itself under the full operation of the blood, there God dwells and there His salvation is experienced.

The blood makes it possible to practice fellowship with God and the Lamb – the Lord Jesus Himself. Have we forgotten His word: *He that eats my flesh and drinks my blood abides in me, and I in him* (John 6:56)? The full blessing of the power of the blood is complete abiding union with Jesus. Only our unbelief separates the work from the person and the blood from the Lord Jesus. He is the One who cleanses by His blood, brings us near, and causes us to drink. Only through the blood are we fitted for complete fellowship with Jesus in heaven as with the Father.

You can see what is needed to mold you for heaven and make you heavenly minded. See that the blood, which always has a place at the throne of grace, demonstrates its power in your hearts, and your lives will become an unbroken fellowship with God and the Lamb – the foretaste of life in eternal glory. Let this thought enter into your soul: the blood already grants in the heart, here on earth, the blessedness of heaven. The precious blood makes life on earth and life in heaven one.

Details for the Song of Heaven

What we have said so far has been taken from what the elder stated about the redeemed. But to what extent is this their experience and testimony? Have we anything out of their own mouths concerning this? Yes, they themselves bear witness. In the song contained in our text, they were heard to cry with loud voice, *Salvation unto him who is seated upon the throne of our God and unto the Lamb.* The Lord Jesus is in the midst of the throne as the slain Lamb, as a Lamb whose blood had been shed. As such, He is the object of the worship of the redeemed.

This appears more clearly in the new song that they sing, *Thou art worthy to take the book and to open its seals, for thou wast slain and hast redeemed us unto God by thy blood, out of every kindred and tongue and nation and hast made us unto our God kings and priests* (Revelation 5:9-10).

It also appears in the apostle's words in the beginning of the book where he spoke after all that he had seen and heard in heaven concerning the place which the Lamb occupied. At the first mention of the name of the Lord Jesus, John cried out, *Unto him that loved us and washed us from our sins in his own blood and has made us kings and priests unto God and his Father; to him be glory and dominion for ever and ever. Amen* (Revelation 1:5-6).

Without ceasing, the blood of the Lamb continues to be the power to awaken the saved to their song of joy and thanksgiving. In the death on the cross, the sacrifice took place in which He gave Himself for them and won them for Himself. The blood is the eternal seal of what He did and of the love which moved Him to do it. It remains the inexhaustible, overflowing fountain of heavenly bliss.

That we may better understand this, notice the expression, *him that loved us and washed us from our sins with his own blood.* In all our consideration about the blood of Jesus, we have had no occasion to stop there until now. And of all the glorious things given by the blood, this is one of the most glorious – His blood is the sign, the measure, and the impartation of His love. Each application of His blood, each time that He causes the soul to experience its power, a fresh outflowing of His wonderful love occurs. The full experience of the power of the blood in eternity will be nothing else than the complete revelation of how He gave Himself for us and gives Himself to us in an eternal, unending, incomprehensible love, as God Himself.

Him that loved us and washed us from our sins with his own blood. This love is indeed incomprehensible. What hasn't that love moved Him to do? He gave Himself for us; He became sin for us; He was made a curse for us. Who would dare to use such language; who could ever have dared to think such a thing if God had not revealed it to us by His Spirit? That He really gave Himself for us, not because it was laid upon Him to do so, but by the impulse of a love that longed for us that we might be identified with Him forever. *But God increased the price of his charity* [love] *toward us in that while we were yet sinners the Christ died for us* (Romans 5:8).

Because it is such a divine wonder, we feel it so little. But, blessed be the Lord! There is a time coming when we shall feel it. Under the ceaseless and immediate love-sharing of the heavenly life, we shall be filled and satisfied with that love. Yes, even here on earth, there is hope that through a better knowledge of and more perfect trust in the blood, the Spirit will more powerfully shed the love of God in our hearts. Nothing can prevent our hearts from being filled with the love of the Lamb and our mouths filled with His praise here on earth as is done in heaven by sight. Each experience of the power of the blood will become increasingly an experience of the love of Jesus.

It has been said that it is not desirable to put too much emphasis on the word *blood*, because it sounds coarse, and the thought expressed by it can be conveyed in a way more in accordance with our modern habit of speaking or thinking.

I must acknowledge that I do not share in this view. I receive that word as coming not just from John, but from the Lord Himself. I am convinced that the word chosen by the Spirit of God and made living and filled with the power of that eternal life carries a power of blessing that surpasses our understanding. Changing the expression into our way of thinking has all the imperfection of a human translation. He who desires to know and experience *what the Spirit saith unto the congregations* will accept the word by faith as having come from heaven as the word containing the joy and power of eternal life. Those expressions, *thy blood* and *the blood of the* Lamb, will make the Holiest, the place of God's glory, resound eternally with the joyful notes of the *new song*.

Heavenly joy through the blood of the Lamb will be the portion of all who with undivided hearts yield to its power. It will also be the portion of all in heaven who have become worthy to take a place among the multitude around the throne.

We have learned what those in heaven say and how they sing about the blood. Let us pray that these tidings may have the effect on us that our Lord intended. To live a real heavenly life, we must abide in the full power of the blood. The blood gives us the right to enter heaven.

As the blood of reconciliation, it works out the full, living consciousness which belongs to those who are at home in heaven. It brings us into the Holiest – near to God. It makes us fit for heaven.

As the cleansing blood, it delivers from the lust and power of sin and preserves us in the fellowship of the light and life of the Holy God. The blood inspires the song of praise in heaven. As the blood of the Lamb who loved us and gave himself for us, it speaks not only of what He has done for us, but also of

Him who has done it all. In the blood, we have the most perfect impartation of Himself. He, who by faith gives himself up to experience completely what the blood is able to do, will soon find an entrance into a life of happy singing of praise and love that heaven alone can surpass.

This life is for you and me. May the blood be all our glory, not only at the cross but also at the throne. Let us plunge deep into the living fountain of the blood of the Lamb. Let us open our hearts wide for its operation. Let us firmly believe in the ceaseless cleansing by which the eternal Priest Himself will apply that blood to us. Let us pray with burning desire that nothing may be in our heart that does not experience the power of the blood. Let us unite joyfully in the song of the great multitude, who know of nothing so glorious as *Thou hast redeemed us unto God by thy blood* (Revelation 5:9).

May our life on earth become what it ought to be – one ceaseless song to Him *that loved us and washed us from our sins in his own blood and has made us kings and priests unto God and his Father; to him be the glory and dominion for ever and ever. Amen* (Revelation 1:5-6).

About the Author

Andrew Murray (1828-1917) was a well-known South African writer, teacher, and pastor. More than two million copies of his books have been sold, and his name is mentioned among other great leaders of the past, such as Charles Spurgeon, T. Austin-Sparks, George Muller, D. L. Moody, and more.

Other Updated Classics, by:

Absolute Surrender, by Andrew Murray

"My God, I am willing that You would make me willing."

God waits to bless us in a way beyond what we expect. From the beginning, ear has not heard, neither has the eye seen, what God has prepared for those who wait for Him (Isaiah 64:4). God has prepared unheard of things, things you never can think of, blessings much more wonderful than you can imagine and mightier than you can conceive. They are divine blessings. Oh, come at once and say, "I give myself absolutely to God, to His will, to do only what God wants." God will enable you to carry out the surrender necessary, if you come to Him with a sincere heart.

Available where books are sold.

Divine Healing, by Andrew Murray

Jesus is still He who heals both soul and body. Salvation offers holiness and healing, and the Holy Spirit is willing to give us a manifestation of His power. When we ask why this divine power is not more often seen, the only biblical answer to be found is: "Because of your unbelief."

Health as well as salvation is to be obtained by faith. The natural tendency of man is to bring about his salvation by his works, and it is only with difficulty that he comes to receive it by faith. But when it is a question of healing the body, he has still more difficulty grasping that truth. As to salvation, he finally accepts it because there is no other way to open the door of heaven. But for the body, he makes use of many other treatments. But happy is he who understands that it is the will of God to show the power of Jesus and to reveal to us His Fatherly love by healing physically as well as spiritually. By doing so, He increases and confirms our faith and teaches us that He demonstrates the power of redemption in the body as well as in the soul.

This book provides biblical clarity concerning divine healing, and supplies basic and applicable principles necessary to having faith concerning healing. The author makes it very clear that we are not healed based on who we are, but based on who Christ is.

Available where books are sold.

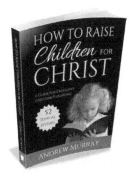

How to Raise Children for Christ, by Andrew Murray

I will put my trust in Him ... Behold I and the children which God has given me – Hebrews 2:13

This book is different from most books on raising children. It is a plea for the parents to truly know and walk with God – for them to love God and His Word. In the correct order, focusing first on the parents, Andrew Murray then urges parents to sincerely and consistently love their children and in all tenderness and gentleness teach them as God also teaches us.

Children are a most precious gift that we receive from God, and they deserve our very best. Our faithful training will not be lost on our children; this is a promise found over and over again in the Scriptures. If our hearts are right towards God and our children, the world's influence will not impact our children. We can and must exercise faith, so our children and our children's children will be able to impact the world for Christ and inherit eternal blessings.

Available where books are sold.

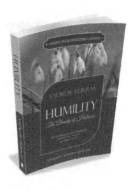

Humility, by Andrew Murray

Is humility a Christlike attribute that should be pursued? And even if it should be, can genuine humility actually be attained? Often so practical in application that it is overlooked, the answer is found by studying the life and words of Christ (*whosoever will be chief among you, let him be your slave*). This little book is a loud call to all committed Christians to prove that meekness and lowliness of heart is the evidence by which those who follow the meek and lowly Lamb of God are to be known. Never mind that your initial efforts will be misunderstood, taken advantage of, or even resisted. Instead, learn from the One who *came not to be ministered unto, but to serve*. For a Christian to be alive, for the life of Christ to reign in and through us, we must be empty of ourselves, exchanging our life for His life, our pride for true, Christlike humility.

Available where books are sold.

The Ministry of Intercession, by Andrew Murray

If the answer to prayer is so positively promised in scripture, why are there so many unanswered prayers today (often mis-interpreted as a "no")? Scripture teaches us that answer to prayer depends upon certain conditions. Christ spoke of faith, of perseverance, of praying in His name, of praying in the will of God. But all these conditions were summed up in the one central statement: *If ye abide in me and my words abide in you, ye shall ask what ye will, and it shall be done unto you.* It becomes clear that the power to pray the effectual prayer of faith depends upon the life.

Let Andrew Murray show you what it means to live in Christ, and let his challenge for genuine intercessory prayer change your life – and the lives of those you are praying for.

Available where books are sold.

Made in the USA
Middletown, DE
30 April 2019